Clin

DECISION MAKING

FOR
Skill-Acquisition
PROGRAMS

Published by Mindstir Media, LLC
45 Lafayette Rd | Suite 181| North Hampton, NH 03862 | USA
1.800.767.0531 | www.mindstirmedia.com

Printed in the United States of America
ISBN-13: 978-1-7334732-7-9
Library of Congress Control Number: 2019913261

Clinical
DECISION
MAKING
FOR
Skill-Acquisition
PROGRAMS

ERICA S. JOWETT HIRST, PH.D., BCBA-D

FOREWORD BY AMBER VALENTINO, PSY.D., BCBA-D

MINDSTIR MEDIA

TABLE OF CONTENTS

FOREWORD

DECISIONS, DECISIONS, DECISIONS. When you work with individuals with autism and other developmental disabilities, you make dozens of them, for each of your learners, every day. I fondly remember my first years as a behavior analyst, working with young children with autism. I can remember coming home at night and agonizing over the decisions I needed to make. I felt an incredible amount of pressure knowing that each decision I made would greatly influence the lives of those I worked with. And, depending on which decision I made, I could either positively or negatively influence clinical outcomes.

"What if I choose the wrong skill to teach next?"
"What if I master something too quickly?"
"What if I forget to teach an important prerequisite skill?"

I wish Dr. Jowett Hirst's book existed back then! Erica and I first became acquainted approximately 5 years ago when she joined a large clinical organization where I was employed after she obtained her Ph.D. from the University of Kansas. Erica displayed excellent decision-making skills and clinical judgment. After her time as a full-time practitioner, I was elated to see her move on to academia where she could apply her clinical skills and develop the clinical repertoires of the next generation of behavior analysts. When she reached out to me about this book, it seemed to be a natural extension of the work she had been doing and a great contribution to our field.

Almost 15 years after my early work as a behavior analyst, I now mentor and teach early career practitioners and see that all too familiar anxiety around decision making that I once had. I am excited to share this resource with my mentees and know that they will have more guidance on making those critical daily decisions than I had in my early career. It is comforting knowing that the guidance from this book will indeed positively influence the lives of their learners. *Clinical Decision Making for Skill-Acquisition Programs* offers practical suggestions for practitioners around skill selection, discrete trial teaching, data-based decision making, and troubleshooting lack of progress. It includes easy to use checklists, specific instructions on when to move on, several options for making various decisions, and reviews after each section to confirm the reader's knowledge of content. I hope every practitioner reads and uses this workbook. And, I hope by doing so, they feel a lessened sense of anxiety and feel supported when making those daily difficult decisions.

Happy Decision Making!

Sincerely,
Amber L. Valentino Psy.D., BCBA-D

PREFACE

THE NUMBER OF INDIVIDUALS receiving applied-behavior-analysis (ABA) services has grown in recent years, and the training obtained by those who work with individuals with developmental disabilities not only varies but may be limited. In addition, the widespread dissemination of assessments and curricula such as Mark Sundberg's Verbal Behavior Milestones Assessment and Placement Program, James Partington's Assessment of Basic Language and Learning Skills-Revised, and Mark Dixon's Promoting the Emergence of Advanced Knowledge has left practitioners with valuable, yet incomplete resources. Therefore, the purpose of this book is to provide guidelines for ABA practitioners as well as those working with individuals with developmental disabilities (e.g., special education teachers) to make meaningful decisions regarding skill selection, one-on-one teaching structure, and program changes, in order to maximize the effectiveness of their work.

Disclaimer: All learner characteristics and information,
assessment results, data, and scenarios are fictional,
and any similarity to an actual person is not intended.

ACKNOWLEDGMENTS

I FIRST WANT TO RECOGNIZE important behavior analysts that have significantly contributed to my understanding of behavior analysis and its clinical application including my doctoral advisor, Claudia Dozier, other major professors (Matthew Normand and Pamela Neidert), clinical supervisors (Leslie Morrison, Traci Cihon, Julie Hardy, Trish Rich, and Christi Reed), and undergraduate internship supervisor (Caio Miguel).

Second, I want to give special thanks to Jana Sarno for providing feedback on early drafts of this workbook. Her detailed review resulted in valuable additions. In addition, several other Board Certified Behavior Analysts provided meaningful comments toward final touches to this workbook.

Finally, I want to thank my husband, Jason Hirst, for his continued encouragement and support during the writing of this workbook.

PART 1

SKILL SELECTION

GIVEN THAT INDIVIDUALS receiving services typically already have delayed skill repertoires, may have difficulty learning, and are not frequently afforded much time for individualized teaching, selecting which skills to teach is just as important as how you teach the skills. However, skills are often selected simply because they come next in a list of skills outlined in an assessment or curriculum, and other times, skills are selected because caregivers (e.g., parents, teachers, staff) request a skill be targeted, or an Individualized Education Plan (IEP) specifies a goal; and in some cases, there is little reasoning behind skill selection. Given the importance of skill selection for the reasons mentioned above, careful consideration should be given to selecting skills. This section will cover essential skills important for any learner receiving services and considerations for learner characteristics and instructional resources.

THE ESSENTIALS

Before selecting target skills from an assessment or curriculum, it is important to teach prerequisite skills necessary for learning as well as basic skills that allow the individual to contact reinforcement. Below are several skills to consider teaching before starting formal teaching sessions (e.g., Discrete Trial Teaching; DTT).

The learner:
1. willingly approaches the instructor
2. accepts a limited amount of reinforcement without exhibiting problem behavior
3. relinquishes access to a preferred item with little problem behavior
4. waits for a reinforcer to be delivered without exhibiting problem behavior
5. attends to (looks at) the instructor and stimuli
6. waits for the instructor without touching teaching materials
7. responds to a variety of prompts (e.g., gestural, model, physical) and does not exhibit problem behavior
8. is able to request preferred items and activities as well as to terminate a non-preferred activity
9. is able to comply with simple instructions

After reading through these skills, you may realize that a current learner for whom you have already begun formal teaching does not possess many of these skills—no need to worry! You can always put current programs on hold and go back to the basics. In the next section, these skills are described, and detail regarding how to teach these skills is outlined. In addition, a checklist of the essentials is available in Appendix A.

1. Approaching the Instructor

Before working with any learner, it is important that the learner feels comfortable with the instructor. When the learner and instructor have a good rapport, the learner will likely be more willing to participate in the learning sessions, and the instructor himself may then function as a reinforcer (i.e., interactions may serve to increase motivation and learning) or the instructor may even be able to make other items reinforcing due to pairing (i.e., the instructor is able to make things fun). Although approaching the instructor is the ideal circumstance, at minimum, the learner should not move away when the instructor moves close to the learner. That is, the instructor should be able to sit within a couple of feet of the learner while the learner remains in the same place. To accomplish this goal, consider the following steps.

- Gather a variety of potentially preferred items.
- Give preferred items to the learner as often as possible.
- Sit near the learner, but do not interact until the learner initiates interaction or tolerates your presence.

  Do NOT
  - take away anything the learner has in possession.
  - deliver any instructions.
  - do anything that evokes any problem or avoidant behavior (e.g., crying, pushing you away, turning away, walking away).

Moving on:
When the learner is consistently approaching you (or tolerating your presence), start to reduce the number of preferred items you are giving the learner. See the next section for details.

2. Tolerating Limited Reinforcement

To effectively teach skills, rewards must be withheld and delivered in small quantities, so that the learner is motivated to learn. However, some learners have a history of accessing large quantities of preferred items and activities, which can be problematic when attempting to deliver a smaller quantity. For example, if a learner is used to being handed a bowl of chips, he will likely become upset when receiving just a piece of one chip, and problem behaviors that emerge as a result of limited reinforcement may interfere with teaching. Therefore, it is important to work with the learner on tolerating limited amounts of reinforcement. To accomplish this goal, consider the following steps.

- Start by giving a little less of the preferred item (e.g., a bowl half filled with chips, a bin with half of the toy trains, five Skittles out of the mini-bag of 20) and ignore any problem behavior that accompanies the reduced access.
- When the learner is readily accepting the lesser amount, give the learner one whole piece of the preferred item (e.g., one chip, one train, one Skittle) and keep giving one after another, again ignoring any problem behavior that accompanies reduced access.
- When the learner is readily accepting the one piece, give the learner part of the whole (if possible; break a chip in half, cut the Skittle in half), again ignoring any problem behavior that accompanies reduced access.

Moving on:
When the learner is consistently accepting small amounts of the reinforcer, start requiring that the learner give non-consumable items back to you. See the next section for details.

3. Giving up the Reinforcer

After the learner has learned to accept a small amount of the reinforcer, it will be important that the learner can give up the reinforcer so that you can use it as a reinforcer for a variety of teaching trials. If removal of the reinforcer evokes problem behavior, this will interfere with learning trials. To accomplish this goal, consider either of the following options.

Option 1

- While sitting near the learner, talk about the item he is playing with and briefly touch the item, ignoring any problem behavior. (If you are unable to sit near the learner, see Step 1)
- When the learner tolerates you briefly touching the item, briefly interact with the item while the learner is holding it (push a button, pull a lever, rotate the item), but do not take the item, and ignore any problem behavior.
- When the learner tolerates you interacting with the item, say, "Let me see this real quick," (or something similar) and pull the item away, giving it back immediately so that the learner doesn't have the opportunity to become upset, and ignore any problem behavior.
- When the learner tolerates you taking the item and immediately giving it back, ask the learner to give it to you. If the learner gives it to you (puts it in your hand), say, "Thanks," and immediately give it back. If the learner does not give it to you, use physical prompting to have the learner give you the item, then immediately give it back. Ignore problem behavior.

Note: Be sure to let the learner have a reasonable amount of time (30 seconds – 1 minute) to access the item between interacting or removing the item and do not run too many trials back-to-back.

See additional option on the next page.

Option 2

- Present the learner with a variety of items (high and low preferred and non-preferred) and wait to see what the learner wants to interact with.
- Once the learner has selected a preferred item to interact with, ask the learner to give you a non-preferred item that he is not interacting with. If the learner does not hand you the item, try pointing to the item or modeling picking up the item. If possible, deliver a consumable reward (a small piece of candy) for giving you the item. In addition, give the item back to the individual after a few seconds. If the individual pushes the item away or does not take it, simply place it near the learner.
- Once the learner is reliably handing you a non-preferred item, repeat the previous step with a preferred item that the learner is not currently interacting with.
- Once the learner is reliably handing you a preferred item that he is not interacting with, repeat the above steps with the item that he is interacting with.

Moving on:
When the learner is consistently giving you the reinforcer, start requiring that the learner wait to access the item. See the next section for details.

4. Waiting for a Reinforcer

Next, because you will be using access to preferred items as reinforcers, you want to ensure that the learner is able to wait for access to the reinforcer. That is, you first need to train waiting for the reinforcer because during a teaching session, you will be asking the learner to do something that requires effort in addition to waiting. To accomplish this goal, consider the following steps.

- Start by immediately giving the learner a non-consumable reinforcer and a small amount of a consumable reinforcer. Do not remove the non-consumable item but continue to give small amounts of the consumable item.
- After a maximum of three "freebies" of the consumable item, tell the learner to "wait" and provide a 1-second delay before giving the item to the learner. If problem behavior occurs at any time, wait to deliver the item until the learner is calm and decrease subsequent delays.
- When the learner can wait for 1 second, increase the delay to 2 seconds. If problem behavior occurs at any time, wait to deliver the item until the learner is calm and decrease subsequent delays.
- As the learner is successful, increase the delays as follows:
  - 3 seconds, 5 seconds, 10 seconds
- When the learner is successfully waiting for 10 seconds, remove access to the non-consumable, so that the learner is waiting without an alternative and repeat the procedures above, giving both the non-consumable and consumable item at the time of delivery.

Note: Do not run too many trials back-to-back.

Moving on:
When the learner is able to wait for at least 10 seconds without exhibiting problem behavior, teach the learner to wait for an instruction. See the next section for details.

5. Waiting for the Instruction

Next, because some (and likely many) of your learning trials will involve stimuli, it is important the learner demonstrates "quiet" or "ready" hands and does not touch the stimuli before an instruction has been presented. This will help reduce pre-guessing and distraction which may interfere with the learning trials. To accomplish this goal, consider the following steps.

- Place one item (non-preferred picture or object) in front of the learner.
- Block touching and reaching for the picture and say, "Wait."
- If needed, prompt the learner to put his hands in his lap or on the table.
- At the moment the learner is not attempting to touch the item, deliver a reinforcer, and remove the item.
- Repeat the steps above until the learner does not attempt to touch the item, then add two and three instructional materials, repeating the steps above.

Moving on:
When the learner is able to wait without touching materials, begin teaching attending. See the next section for details.

6. Attending to Stimuli and the Instructor

Next, you want the learner to be able to attend to (i.e., look at) the stimuli to be used for teaching as well as the instructor. When a learner has good attention to the stimuli and instructor, he is more likely to respond correctly and learn faster. To accomplish this goal, consider the following steps for each skill.

Attending to stimuli
- Hold up an item (picture or object) in front of the learner.
- If the learner looks at the item within 3 seconds, deliver a reinforcer. If the learner does not look at the item within 3 seconds, say, "Look here," (or something similar), shake the item, and/or block looking away.
- Once the learner is consistently looking at the item presented directly in front of him, present an item to the side of the learner, and use the steps outlined above.
- Once the learner is consistently looking at items presented to either side of the learner, present items above and below the learner's natural line of sight and use the steps outlined above.

Attending to an instructor
- While sitting directly in front of the learner in close proximity, call the learner's name or say, "Watch me," while performing an action such as clapping your hands or waving.
- If the learner looks at what the instructor is doing within 3 seconds, deliver a reinforcer. If the learner does not look at the instructor within 3 seconds, repeat the instruction and block looking away.
- Note that the learner does not need to make eye contact but needs to be able to orient toward the instructor.
- If you are having difficulty getting the learner to attend to the instructor, consider using interesting objects or minimal physical guidance* as needed (e.g., place fingers under the chin to direct face toward the instructor or place a hand on the side of the head

and gently orient the learner toward the instructor). In addition, you may want to reinforce spontaneous attending until the learner is consistently orienting toward the instructor, then attempt to repeat the initial steps above.

*If the learner is exhibiting challenging behaviors in response to physical prompting, see Step 7 regarding *allowing a physical prompt.*

Moving on:
When the learner is able to attend to the stimuli and instructor, begin teaching response to prompts. See the next section for details.

7. Responding to Prompts

To teach any skill, it will be necessary to provide prompts; however, a prompt is only effective if the learner is able to respond correctly to that prompt. For example, if an instructor is pointing to a specific object in an array, the learner needs to be able to respond by touching the corresponding item. In another example, if an instructor is demonstrating how to clap hands, the learner must be able to imitate the action of clapping. To accomplish this goal, consider the following steps.

Allowing a physical prompt
- Briefly touch the learner's hand and then deliver a reinforcer. Ignore any problem behavior.
- When the learner is consistently allowing you to touch his hand and is not engaging in any problematic behavior, briefly pick up the learner's hand and then immediately release it and deliver a reinforcer. Ignore any problem behavior.
- When the learner is consistently allowing you to pick up his hand, pick up the learner's hand and put it on an object or picture. Repeating the procedures above.
- When the learner is consistently allowing you to pick up his hand and put it on an item, pick up the learner's hand and guide an action (e.g., waving, pointing), repeating the procedures above.
- You may also consider using this procedure to desensitize the learner to other physical prompts such as moving the learner from one point to another or guiding other actions such as lifting the leg or turning the head.

Following a point prompt
- Place three items (objects or pictures) in front of the learner.
- Point to one of the three items and say, "Touch this one."
- If the learner touches the item within 3 seconds, deliver a reinforcer. If the learner does not touch the item within 3 seconds, use physical guidance to have the learner touch the item and repeat.

- Repeat this procedure until the learner is following the point prompt consistently regardless of which item you point to.
- Note that the learner does not need to point (you can teach this as a skill in the future).

Imitating Actions

- Start by performing a simple action such as raising your hand and say, "Do this."
- If the learner performs or approximates the action, deliver a reinforcer. If the learner does not attempt to approximate the action, ensure the learner is attending, repeat the instruction, and provide a physical prompt.
- Repeat this procedure with different simple actions until the learner is readily attempting the actions.

Moving on:

When the learner is consistently following prompts, begin working on manding. See the next section for details.

8. Manding

Regardless of your learner's age or level of support needs, manding (or requesting) will be essential. Manding gives the individual control over his environment and an effective way to access reinforcers. Having a manding repertoire is especially important for two reasons. First, the individual experiences the value of language, which makes it more likely that he will learn other communicative responses. Second, having the ability to verbally communicate reduces the likelihood that the individual will engage in problematic behaviors as a form of communication.

Before beginning mand training, it is important to select an appropriate mode of communication. If the learner is able to vocally imitate sounds or words, vocal speech should be targeted. However, although vocal speech is the most universal, it is not the best option for every learner. If the learner is not able to vocally imitate, the instructor should consider using sign language, picture exchange, or an augmentative/alternative communication (AAC) device.

Learners with Vocal Abilities

For learners who are able to imitate vocalizations, it is important to target mands that are achievable. If the learner can only imitate sounds, then first target only one sound (e.g., "/k/" for cookie). Also, be sure to select a sound that the learner already has in his repertoire or is otherwise developmentally appropriate. For example, if the learner can't say "/k/," for cookie, but can say, "ee," start with that part of the word. As the learner masters one sound, increase to two syllables, etc. When including syllables that are not yet in the learner's repertoire, be sure to determine whether the sound is developmentally appropriate. If the learner can imitate words, first target one-word mands using the name of the item that is being requested (e.g., cookie, swing). As the learner masters one-word mands, increase to two words, etc.

With respect to adding words, consider the importance of the words for the learner. Common words and phrases to add are "I want," "Can I have," and "Please;" and characteristics of your learner should determine which words/phrases are added. It is very common for instructors to first add "Please," then teach "I want" phrases, and these are appropriate for individuals with minimal support needs because they tend to learn quickly. Therefore, teaching additional phrases is relatively easy. However, learners with intensive support needs tend to require many teaching trials, and "Please" is not very functional; therefore, consider starting with the more desirable phrase first ("Can I have") and backward chaining. That is, after teaching the one-word mand (e.g., cookie), next target "have (item)," followed by "I have (item)," then "Can I have (item)?"

Learners without Vocal Abilities

Considerations for learners with intensive support needs. For learners with very few skills who do not express vocal abilities, picture exchange and simple augmentative communication are preferable. Teaching picture exchange is relatively easy because the motor movement involved is simple (i.e., pointing to or handing someone a card) and constant. Another benefit to using pictures is that pictures are universally recognized which will allow the learner to be more successful in communicating with those around him. That being said, it is important to be mindful when selecting pictures to be used. When possible, pictures of the actual items should be used so that it is easy for the learner to learn with what item/activity the picture corresponds and those who interact with the learner will be able to easily recognize the item/activity being requested. For learners who engage in destructive behaviors, consider an augmentative communication device that is durable (e.g., tablet in protective cover).

Considerations for learners with minimal support needs. For learners who have minimal support needs and who are integrated into environments with typical peers, but do not express vocal abilities, consider sign language or advanced augmentative communication. Sign language is appropriate for individuals who are preparing for integration into a signing community, and advanced AAC devices (text-to-speech) are appropriate for those who will not be in a signing community so that they can be understood by others in the environment.

Regardless of the mode of communication, if a learner is capable of producing any sounds, be sure to work on reinforcing speech sounds.

Teaching Manding

Regardless of the mode of communication, below are some general steps for teaching an individual to mand.

Requesting something preferred
- Withhold access to a highly preferred item/activity and wait 5 seconds.
- If the individual requests the item/activity, provide brief access (15-30 seconds). If the individual does not request the item, prompt the desired behavior (e.g., point to the card, physically guide the correct sign, model the vocalization).
- Continue practicing using these steps until the individual can request independently (without prompts).
- Once the individual is consistently requesting an item/activity, work on requesting to terminate the presence of an item or ongoing activity.

Requesting to terminate something aversive
- Present a non-preferred item (e.g., edible) and ask, "Do you want this?" or start a non-preferred activity (e.g., deliver an instruction to complete a task) and wait 5 seconds.
- If the individual communicates that he doesn't want the item (e.g., says, "No," signs No) or wants to stop the activity (e.g., asks for a break, exchanges the stop card), remove the item or discontinue the activity for 15 seconds. If the individual does not request to terminate the aversive event, use prompting strategies previously outlined.
- Repeat opportunities for practice until the individual can request to terminate something aversive without prompts.

Moving on:
When the learner is consistently manding, work on compliance with simple, functional instructions. See the next section for details.

9. Demonstrating Simple Compliance

Because you will eventually be working on skills that are challenging for the learner, it is important to be sure that the learner will comply with simple, known instructions (e.g., motor imitation, one-step instructions) that require minimal effort. If the learner does not comply with simple instructions, the likelihood of noncompliance during individualized instruction will be high. A few important basic skills are listed below.

- Learner will walk to the instructor when instructed to come here.
- Learner will sit down on the floor or chair when asked to sit here.
- Learner will point to and give a known item to the instructor.

See teaching techniques mentioned in previous sections for working on skills listed above.

Moving on:
After the learner has learned these essential skills, you are ready to select curricular, social, and/or functional living skills. The next section will outline important considerations for selecting skills.

IMPORTANT CONSIDERATIONS

After ensuring that the learner has the essential skills for learning and you are ready to select skills for individualized instruction, several considerations should guide your decision for selecting skills.

- **Is the skill age appropriate?**
  To determine if a skill is age appropriate, consider whether same-age peers exhibit the skill.

- **Will the skill be useful for the learner?**
  To determine if the skill will be useful for the learner, consider how often the learner will use the skill or what types of reinforcers the learner will be able to access when using the skill, regardless of whether the skill is age appropriate.

- **Does the learner have the necessary prerequisite skills?**
  To determine if the learner has the necessary prerequisite skills, consider the behaviors needed to learn the new skill.

- **Is the skill a prerequisite skill for other important skills?**
  Although the skill itself might not be important in and of itself, it would be an important skill if it will lead to the acquisition of other skills.

- **Is the skill important to the caregiver or learner?**
  Even if a specific skill doesn't seem to have utility, it may simply be a skill that is important to the caregiver or learner, which is also important to consider.

- **Is the skill likely to be maintained in the natural environment?**
  Consider whether the skill will be effective outside of the teaching environment.

- **Are the necessary resources available?**
  Consider whether the necessary resources (staff, teaching materials) are readily available.

If you can answer, "Yes" to these questions, the skill should be considered for teaching. In the next section, you will learn some additional considerations for selecting skills depending on the level of support needs of the individual.

Considerations for Learners with Intensive Support Needs

Below are a few general considerations for learners who have repertoires far below same-age peers, tend to acquire skills very slowly, require a high degree of prompting, and require several teaching trials to master a skill.

- **Start basic independent living and self-care skills early**

  Because learners with intensive support needs tend to acquire skills slowly, it is important to consider teaching skills early that will be needed in the future. Although a young learner is likely living at home under the care of an adult, it is important to start working on basic independent-living and self-care skills (e.g., toileting, dressing, showering) early—perhaps as early as middle school—so that he requires as little assistance as possible with daily activities as an adult.

- **Discontinue academics with older children**

  It is all too common for children's IEPs to specify academic goals because the child is still in school. However, if the child has intensive support needs and has acquired few skills toward the end of middle school/beginning of high school, academic skills are likely no longer important as they won't be useful for the individual in adulthood. That is, if the individual has not learned basic reading, writing, and math by this point, it is unlikely that he will acquire these skills to the degree to which they would be useful. That being said, there may be a few useful skills to teach that are considered "academic" such as recognizing and writing one's own name.

- **Ensure a variety of leisure skills**

  Because most individuals with intensive support needs will not hold a full-time engaging job and will likely spend most of their day at home or in a residential setting with limited activities, it is important to give the individual skills necessary to keep himself occupied.

Considerations for Learners with Minimal Support Needs

Below are a few general considerations for learners who have repertoires encompassing several skills of a same-age peer, require minimal prompting, and tend to acquire skills readily with few teaching trials to mastery.

- **Try to keep academic performance at the rate of peers**
  Because individuals with minimal support needs are likely participating in a mainstream classroom, it is important to maintain academic performance of same-age peers so that the individual can continue interacting with this peer group. When an individual falls too far behind same-age peers, the individual is typically placed in a special education environment where there will be fewer appropriate peer models and opportunities for social-skill development.

- **Start training for vocational skills before leaving high school**
  Individuals with minimal support needs are likely those who will hold at least a part-time job as an adult; however, due to their disabilities, it may take more effort than standard on-the-job training to teach them the skills necessary for a given job. Therefore, it is important to start teaching vocational (work skills) early to ensure gainful employment.

- **Ensure advanced independent-living and self-care skills**
  Also consider that an individual who has minimal support needs is likely to live independently as an adult or with minimal assistance (assisted living); therefore, you want to target advanced independent-living and self-care skills (laundry, dishes, handling money, brushing teeth) to decrease the degree to which he is reliant on others.

Determining Number of Targets

Now that you've learned some important considerations for what skills to select, next consider *how many* skills you will select to work on. Below are some general guidelines.

- **Level of support needs**
  Learners with higher support needs should have fewer targets; whereas, learners with lower support needs should have more targets.

- **Number of hours of instruction per week**
  Learners receiving few hours of instruction per week (e.g., 6 hours) should have few targets; whereas, learners receiving many hours (e.g., 20+) can have several targets.

- **Level of compliance/interfering problem behavior**
  Learners with higher levels of interfering problem behavior should have few targets; whereas, learners who demonstrate high levels of compliance should have more targets.

- **Number of programs**
  Learners working on skills in several domains (five or more programs) should have few targets per program; whereas, learners working on skills in few domains (three or fewer programs) could have more targets in each program.

- **Instructor fluency**
  Learners who have instructors who are very new and/or not yet fluent at conducting trials should have fewer targets; whereas, learners with a fluent instructor can have more targets. If a learner has a variety of instructors with varying levels of fluency, select a few targets for the inexperienced instructor(s) to work on, but have the experienced instructor(s) work on all targets.

- **Length of teaching session**
  Learners with short sessions (e.g., 1 hour) should have fewer targets than learners with long sessions (e.g., 3 hours).

- **Difficulty of programs**
  Fewer targets should be selected for effortful or time-consuming programs (e.g., writing words); whereas, more targets can be selected for easier or less time-consuming programs (e.g., color matching).

The above guidelines are intended as suggestions for selecting skills, and all variables should be taken into consideration.

REVIEW

Which skills are essential for any learner who will be learning new skills?

1. _____

2. _____

3. _____

4. _____

5. _____

6. _____

7. _____

8. _____

9. _____

What should you consider when selecting a new skill?

1. _____

2. _____

3. _____

4. _____

5. _____

6. _____

7. _____

What should you consider when selecting skills for learners with intensive support needs?

1. _____

2. _____

3. _____

What should you consider when selecting skills for learners with minimal support needs?

1. _____

2. _____

3. _____

What factors should influence how many skills you target?

1. _____

2. _____

3. _____

4. _____

5. _____

6. _____

7. _____

PART 2

RECOMMENDED GUIDELINES FOR INDIVIDUALIZED INSTRUCTION

NOW THAT YOU'VE LEARNED how to select appropriate goals for your learner, next, consider how you will structure your learning sessions to maximize learning and reduce errors. The next few sections will cover basic session considerations and appropriate use of error correction, prompting, reinforcement, data collection, and task interspersal.

THE BASICS

Listed below are several considerations for improving the success of your teaching sessions.

- **Have fun!**
  Often times, the focus of the teaching session is about getting through as many targets as possible. Although it's important to provide a sufficient number of learning opportunities, it is also important to remember to have fun. Keeping your session fun will encourage continued rapport between the instructor and learner and help reduce learner and instructor burnout.

- **Mix it up**
  Teaching sessions can become very rote and monotonous which makes the session boring (and maybe even annoying) for the learner, the instructor, and perhaps an observer (e.g., parent, teacher, etc.). In addition, rote teaching may also create rote learning (i.e., lack of generalization). Therefore, consider presenting a variety of instructions, changing up the targets, using at least 10 different praise statements, varying the array of presentation of stimuli, and varying the location of instruction.

- **Speak normally**
  Many instructors (new and seasoned) tend to adopt a teaching style that involves abnormal inflections or emphasis on specific words, which can be problematic if the learner is imitating these abnormalities while learning vocal speech and can also be aversive for the learner or an observer to listen to. Instructional abnormalities can usually be identified by listening to a recording of one's own teaching session or asking a peer to observe one of your teaching sessions. Once identified, instructors should work toward speaking normally as if speaking to a person without a disability.

- **Use common stimuli**

  When using objects (or pictures) in teaching, use stimuli with which the learner is already familiar or stimuli that the learner is likely to encounter. In addition, as briefly mentioned in *Mix it up,* be sure to include multiple exemplars of stimuli. Use of several examples of common stimuli will aid in generalization and be useful for the learner in the long run.

- **Use learner-response-based prompting**

  Many programs involve very specific instructions for prompting (i.e., most-to-least or least-to-most prompting), which are appropriate for some learners. However, changing the use of prompts based on learner responding helps to maximize correct responses and minimize errors. To use learner-response-based prompting, when the learner is responding correctly, reduce the use of prompts, and when the learner is making errors, increase the use of prompts. This type of flexible prompting will be discussed in more detail in later sections.

- **Use an appropriate pace**

  It's all too easy as an instructor to deliver instructions at a rapid pace because you already know what you are teaching the learner, but consider the difficulty for the learner trying to keep up with a pace that is too fast. On the other hand, it is equally important that your rate of instruction is not too slow because you may lose the attention of the learner or may not get in a sufficient number of learning trials which may result in slower skill acquisition.

- **Take breaks often**

  Always keep in mind that it is easier to be the instructor than the learner. Remember what it was like when you were in school—it can be quite mentally exhausting! Therefore, consider that your learner may need a break from learning sooner than you feel he needs a break.

- **Deliver the reinforcer immediately**

  Because data collection is an important part of tracking progress, it's easy for an instructor to record learner responding immediately after the learner responds to an instruction. However, recording creates a delay in delivery of reinforcement, which may reduce the likelihood that the learner will continue responding correctly or at all. Therefore, it is important to ensure immediate delivery of the reinforcer after a correct response.

- **Allow choice of reinforcers**

  To ensure that your learner stays motivated to learn, it is important to allow frequent opportunities to choose reinforcers. Although formal preference assessments identify high-preferred items, they may lose their value over time. Therefore, it is important to frequently assess what the learner is interested in, and this can be done immediately before or immediately following a task/work period. For younger learners or learners with intensive support needs, if you have the learner make a choice before the work period, it is beneficial to allow brief access to the chosen item, so that choice doesn't immediately result in a demand. Alternatively, you can have the learner choose what he wants immediately following a correct response or the end of a work period.

- **Match the reinforcer with the response effort**

  Always keep in mind that some skills are harder than others, either due to effort or time. Because the difficulty of skills varies, it is important to provide a sufficient amount or quality of reinforcer for more difficult skills. That is, more and higher quality reinforcers should be given for more difficult tasks.

- **Structure the environment**

  Many learners can become easily distracted by things in the learning environment as well as can learn quickly how to escape tasks. Therefore, you should be mindful about how the learning environment is structured. To reduce distractions, consider what the learner will see and hear. For example, if you will be placing pictures on a table for the learner to select, the table should not have designs or pictures that make it difficult to scan the teaching stimuli. In another example, you might consider using headphones for other learners watching videos on a tablet, so that your learner is not distracted by the sound. To reduce opportunities for escape and other problem behavior (e.g., aggression), consider the placement of the learner and where you sit. For example, if your learner is likely to exhibit aggression, you might want to stand behind the learner, or if your learner is likely to run away, you might want to sit near the learner to block an attempt to escape or position furniture to make it more difficult for the learner to escape.

ERROR CORRECTION & PROMPTING GUIDELINES

Prompting can be (and is) used in a variety of ways to facilitate skill acquisition. Prompting can be used proactively to evoke correct responding before the learner has an opportunity to error, or reactively as a consequence for no or incorrect responding (later referred to as error correction; EC), and both types of prompting have advantages and disadvantages. When prompting is consistently used proactively, learners have more opportunities to respond correctly and contact reinforcement (see example below). *Note: In all of the following examples, each trial denotes the same target and assumes that other targets are being interspersed.*

Trial 1: instructor **uses immediate prompt,** learner responds **correctly,** and instructor **delivers reinforcer**

Trial 2: instructor **uses immediate prompt,** learner responds **correctly,** and instructor **delivers reinforcer**

Trial 3: instructor **uses immediate prompt,** learner responds **correctly,** and instructor **delivers reinforcer**

Trial 4: instructor **uses immediate prompt,** learner responds **correctly,** and instructor **delivers reinforcer**

Trial 5: instructor **uses immediate prompt,** learner responds **correctly,** and instructor **delivers reinforcer**

In the example above, the learner made 0 errors, responded with 100% accuracy, and earned 100% of available reinforcers. However, the learner may become dependent on the prompts in order to respond correctly. Therefore, prompting may be used reactively to give learners more opportunities to respond independently (see example below).

Trial 1: instructor **does not use a prompt,** learner responds **incorrectly,** instructor implements **error correction,** learner responds **correctly**

Trial 2: instructor **does not use a prompt,** learner responds **incorrectly,** instructor implements **error correction,** learner responds **correctly**

Trial 3: instructor **does not use a prompt,** learner responds **incorrectly,** instructor implements **error correction,** learner responds **correctly**

Trial 4: instructor **does not use a prompt,** learner responds **incorrectly,** instructor implements **error correction,** learner responds **correctly**

Trial 5: instructor **does not use a prompt,** learner responds **incorrectly,** instructor implements **error correction,** learner responds **correctly**

In the example above, the learner made five errors and five correct responses and did not receive any available reinforcers.

For the instructor to maximize correct responding, minimize errors, and reduce the chance for prompt dependency, it is important that the instructor learns to teach based on learner responding. That is, if the learner is responding correctly without a prompt, the instructor should continue to present the instruction without a prompt and work on other teaching targets. However, if the learner is responding incorrectly, the instructor should present a prompt during subsequent trials and provide learning opportunities often. Once the learner is responding correctly with a prompt, the instructor should allow for independent responding by presenting only the instruction. This type of flexibility in prompting allows learners to respond independently more often when they are successfully learning but provides more prompting when the learner is not responding correctly independently. See the example below.

Trial 1: instructor **does not use a prompt,** learner responds **incorrectly,** instructor implements **error correction,** learner responds **correctly**

Trial 2: instructor **uses immediate prompt,** learner responds **correctly,** and instructor **delivers reinforcer**

Trial 3: instructor **does not use a prompt,** learner responds **incorrectly,** instructor implements **error correction,** learner responds **correctly**

Trial 4: instructor **uses immediate prompt,** learner responds **correctly,** and instructor **delivers reinforcer**

Trial 5: instructor **does not use a prompt,** learner responds **correctly,** and instructor **delivers reinforcer**

Trial 6: instructor **does not use a prompt,** learner responds **correctly,** and instructor **delivers reinforcer**

In the example above, the learner had only two errors, responded correctly six times (some of which occurred in the absence of a prompt), and contacted reinforcement four times.

This type of learner-response-based prompting is meant to serve as a general guideline (starting point) and should be modified based on learner responding. In particular, learners with intensive support needs may need more proactive prompts with systematic fading procedures. For example, some learners may need several consecutive trials or sessions using proactive prompting. To determine your learner's progress, see *Data-based Decision Making.* For tips on prompt fading, see *Making Program Changes.*

Additional Considerations for Error Correction

When a learner responds incorrectly, it is usually important (although not always necessary) to provide an immediate prompt so that the learner can practice the correct response. In addition, it is also sometimes important to provide an immediate opportunity to respond in the absence of prompt; however, this decision, like all decisions regarding teaching strategies, should also be learner specific. Below are some points for consideration.

Providing an opportunity to respond independently immediately following a prompted response can be beneficial for individuals who tend to error on subsequent trials when prompts are not used. However, this step may not be necessary for individuals who tend to respond correctly on subsequent trials. In addition, if the individual is responding incorrectly immediately following prompted responses, you may not want to remove prompts on subsequent trials until he has a history of several correct responses on unprompted trials following a prompted trial.

Below is an example of what to do when the learner is responding **correctly** on unprompted trials following a prompted trial.

Trial 1: No prompt → Incorrect → **EC (prompt)** → Correct

Trial 2: **Prompt** → Correct → Reinforce

Trial 3: No prompt → Correct → Reinforce

Trial 4: No prompt → Correct → Reinforce

In the example above, the learner is able to respond correctly in subsequent trials without practicing independently following error correction; therefore, the additional practice immediately following EC is unnecessary.

Below is an example of what to do when the learner is responding **incorrectly** on unprompted trials following a prompted trial.

Trial 1: No prompt → Incorrect → **EC (prompt)** → Correct

Trial 2: **Prompt** → Correct → Reinforce

Trial 3: No prompt → Incorrect → **EC (prompt)** → Correct → **No prompt** → Correct

Trial 4: **Prompt** → Correct → Reinforce → **No prompt** → Correct

Trial 5: No prompt → Correct → Reinforce

In the example above, the learner is not responding correctly during unprompted trials; therefore, you want to fade your prompt within each teaching trial to increase the likelihood that a correct response will occur in the absence of a prompt during subsequent trials.

However, if the learner is not responding correctly when removing the prompt within the trial (see example below), you may want to increase the number of prompted trials.

Trial 1: No prompt → Incorrect → **EC (prompt)** → Correct

Trial 2: Prompt → Correct → Reinforce

Trial 3: No prompt → Incorrect → **EC (prompt)** → Correct → **No prompt** → Incorrect

Trial 4: Prompt → Correct → Reinforce → **No prompt** → Incorrect

Trial 5: Prompt → Correct → Reinforce

Trial 6: Prompt → Correct → Reinforce

Trial 7: Prompt → Correct → Reinforce

REINFORCEMENT GUIDELINES

In general, reinforcers are delivered following correct responses to increase the likelihood of correct responding in the future; however, it is important to deliver reinforcers systematically to maximize their effectiveness. Reinforcers may be delivered 1) following only independent, correct responses, 2) all correct responses (regardless if the correct response was prompted), or 3) a combination of these.

In the first example where reinforcers are delivered only for independent correct responses, this method encourages the learner to respond independently because independent responding is differentially reinforced (i.e., prompted responses are not reinforced). However, if the learner is unable to respond correctly independently, he is not contacting reinforcement, which may delay skill acquisition.

In the second example where reinforcers are delivered for all correct responses, this method allows the learner to contact reinforcement more easily and frequently. However, the learner may become dependent on prompts and lack the motivation to respond independently.

To ensure the individual contacts reinforcement, but does not become dependent on prompts, consider a combination of these procedures based on the learner's **first response**. In the last section, you learned about how to use prompting based on the learner's responding where some trials involve an opportunity for an independent response, and other trials include immediate prompts. Using this method allows for reinforcement of the first correct response. So, if you did not provide a prompt at the start of the trial, the learner must respond independently to earn the reinforcer. However, if you did provide a prompt at the start of the trial, the learner simply needs to respond correctly following the prompt to earn the reinforcer. *(See Sample Teaching Session)*

Additional Considerations for Reinforcement

In addition to determining which responses should be reinforced (independent, prompted, or a combination), also consider how immediately you deliver the reinforcer, how much you deliver, and what types of reinforcers are delivered. Regardless of which responses (independent or prompted) result in the delivery of a reinforcer, it is important to be sure the reinforcer is delivered immediately following the correct response to maximize the effectiveness of the reinforcer.

With respect to how much and what type of reinforcer is delivered, keep in mind that large magnitudes of reinforcement are likely to be of more value than smaller amounts (e.g., five chips vs. one piece of one chip), and some reinforcers will be more valuable than other reinforcers (e.g., iPad vs. stuffed animal). Given these differences in value, you might consider reinforcing both independent and prompted responses, but give more of the reinforcer for independent as compared to prompted. Similarly, you might provide access to the more valuable reinforcer (highest preferred) for independent responding and access to a less valuable (low preferred) reinforcer for prompted responding. In this way, you can still reinforce correct responding, but the reinforcer favors independent responding.

SAMPLE TEACHING SESSION

In the example below, the learner is working on labeling a dog, saying, "three," and imitating clapping hands. Note that the session begins with opportunities for independent responding for all targets, but the instructor provides prompts on subsequent trials when the learner responds incorrectly and removes those prompts when the learner responds correctly. In addition, note that the reinforcer (S^R) is delivered following correct responses if the first response was correct (i.e., reinforcers are not provided if the learner responds correctly during error correction [EC]).

Trial	Instruction	Prompt	Response	Consequence
1	What is it?	none	correct	S^R
2	1, 2...	none	incorrect	EC
3	Do this	none	incorrect	EC
4	1, 2...	**vocal**	correct	S^R
5	Do this	**physical**	correct	S^R
6	1, 2...	none	correct	S^R
7	Do this	none	correct	S^R
8	What is it?	none	correct	S^R
9	1, 2...	none	incorrect	EC
10	Do this	none	correct	S^R
11	1, 2...	**vocal**	correct	S^R
12	What is it?	none	correct	S^R
13	1, 2...	none	correct	S^R
14	Do this	none	correct	S^R
15	1, 2...	none	correct	S^R
16	What is it?	none	correct	S^R
18	Do this	none	correct	S^R
19	1, 2...	none	correct	S^R

Note: In the table above, the instruction for labeling a dog is "What is it?"; the instruction for the intraverbal response "three" is "1, 2..."; and the instruction for imitating clapping hands is "Do this." A vocal prompt is "three" and a physical prompt is guiding the learner's hands together.

DATA COLLECTION

Collecting data is crucial for individualized instruction, and there are two behaviors you should record for a given teaching trial. The most obvious is the learner's behavior—correct, incorrect, or no response. However, another important piece of information to record is whether a prompt was used at the start of the trial. For example, a correct, independent response would be recorded as "+", whereas a correct, prompted response would be recorded as "+P". This information is useful in two ways; it can be used to guide instruction in subsequent trials, and it can be used later to inform decisions regarding what kinds of changes to make to the learner's program. Below is an example of how data would be collected for teaching the learner how to write the letter A.

Teaching Trial	Data
Trial 1: "Write A" → **incorrect** → **EC** → **correct**	-
(Note that even though the learner responded correctly following error correction, a "-" is recorded because that was the first response. This now informs the instructor to use an immediate prompt on the next trial)	
Trial 2: "Write A" plus partial physical prompt → **correct**	+PP
(This now informs the instructor to remove the prompt on the next trial; however, if the learner had a −PP, this would inform the instructor to use a full physical prompt on the next trial)	
Trial 3: "Write A" → **correct**	+

TASK INTERSPERSAL

When structuring your teaching session, it is generally beneficial to use task interspersal by rotating the presentation of various instructions. This can be done in several ways. First, you can rotate acquisition (non-mastered) targets within a given program. See the example below for receptive identification of colors.

Trial 1: "Point to red"
Trial 2: "Point to blue"
Trial 3: "Point to yellow"

The benefit to interspersing tasks within the same program is that the learner must carefully attend to the relevant part of the instruction (i.e., the color). However, for more advanced learners, you can also rotate acquisition targets across multiple programs. See example below.

Trial 1: "Point to red"
Trial 2: "Do this" (clapping)
Trial 3: "What's your name?"

An alternative to interspersing acquisition targets is to intersperse mastered (known) targets as in the example below.

Trial 1 (acquisition): "Point to red"
Trial 2 (mastered): "Touch your head"
Trial 3 (acquisition): "Point to blue"

The decision to intersperse mastered targets into your teaching session warrants several considerations; and one advantage may be that the learner feels more successful (i.e., automatic reinforcement) because he is able to respond correctly more often throughout the session, which may be desirable for some learners. In addition, if the learner is earning reinforcers for correct responses to mastered targets, he is contacting more reinforcement overall, which may improve the learner's or caregiver's overall satisfaction with the teaching sessions and result in fewer challenging behaviors.

Although there are potential advantages to interspersing mastered targets, also consider that interspersing mastered targets has several potential disadvantages. First, if you are delivering reinforcement for mastered targets, this may reduce motivation for responding correctly to acquisition targets. Therefore, if you are interspersing mastered targets, you might consider using a less-preferred reinforcer for the mastered target. Second, repeated presentation of mastered targets may become boring for the learner, which could result in a lack of responding or display of other challenging behaviors. Similarly, presentation of mastered targets creates unnecessary extra work for the learner, which may become aversive over time. Finally, each time a mastered target is presented, the learner is missing an opportunity to work on an acquisition target, which may result in a delay to learning new and important skills given limited time for individualized instruction.

Regardless of whether you are interspersing acquisition or mastered tasks, be sure to vary the order in which you present the instructions so that the learner does not acquire a skill because he can predict the answer. In addition, also consider how many targets are interspersed at a time. For example, when working on a difficult skill, you want to intersperse only one or two targets (or none if the skill needs repeated practice); however, for skills that are easier, you should intersperse several targets before presenting the easy instruction. This will allow you to spend more time working on skills that are challenging for the learner and less time on skills that are easy.

REVIEW

What basic session components should you include in your teaching sessions?

1. _____

2. _____

3. _____

4. _____

5. _____

6. _____

7. _____

8. _____

9. _____

10. _____

11. _____

What are some things you just learned about how to use error correction, prompting, and reinforcement to maximize learning, and how might you incorporate these changes with some of your current learners?

_____

_____

_____

_____

_____

_____

_____

_____

_____

_____

_____

_____

Which behaviors are important to record?

1. _____

2. _____

What are three ways to intersperse targets?

1. _____

2. _____

3. _____

What did you learn are **advantages** of interspersing mastered targets?

1. _____

2. _____

What did you learn are **disadvantages** of interspersing mastered targets?

1. _____

2. _____

3. _____

4. _____

PART 3

DATA-BASED
DECISION MAKING

AMONG MANY IMPORTANT RESPONSIBILITIES, instructors must know when to make intervention changes and what to change. Knowing when to make an intervention change is crucial in order to maximize correct responding and minimize the practice of errors. In the past, you may have learned to wait until you have three or more data points before changing an intervention; or maybe you have tried to wait until behavior was stable before making a change. Although these are good rules in general, especially for empirical evaluation, there are exceptions to these rules.

On the next page, you will see a review of common patterns of responding that will be used in subsequent examples of graphs for which you will learn when to make changes to your interventions.

COMMON PATTERNS OF RESPONDING

Below are examples of a few common patterns of responding you may see during skill-acquisition programs. *Note: Baseline conditions (no intervention) are denoted by BL.*

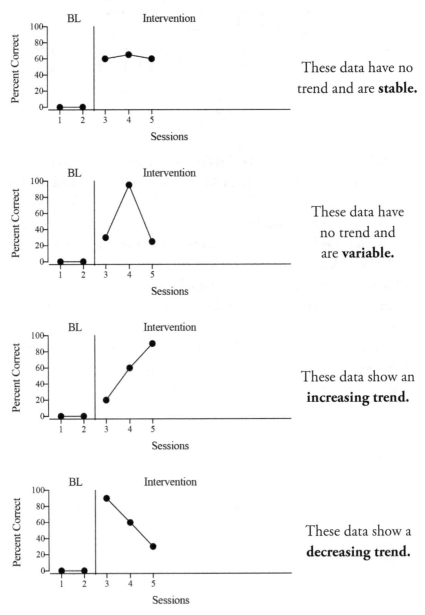

These data have no trend and are **stable.**

These data have no trend and are **variable.**

These data show an **increasing trend.**

These data show a **decreasing trend.**

LEARNING TO MAKE DATA-BASED DECISIONS

The hypothetical graph below provides an all-too-common example of a learner's graph.

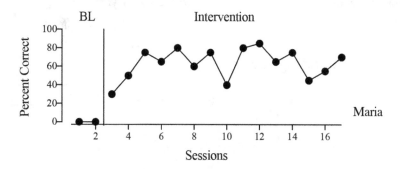

Assume that Maria has two sessions per week. This means she has been responding similarly for nearly 2 months, and no program changes have been made. This lack of decision making may occur because the instructor was not graphing data regularly, or the graph was not being analyzed. Either way, these graphs are problematic for several reasons. First, the learner has been practicing errors for an extended period; and biologically, the practice of a behavior makes it more likely that the behavior will occur again in the future. Second, the time spent working on this skill was at the expense of working on other potentially important skills. And third, the learner is likely tired of working on this same task every session, which may result in decreased compliance or problem behavior over time. Therefore, it is important to be aware of when to make a change, so that action can be taken quickly to ensure the learner is responding correctly as often as possible.

In addition, keep in mind that to make a data-based decision, it is crucial that you are monitoring your learner's data after each session.

In the next section, you will see a variety of patterns of responding you might encounter with your learners and learn when you should continue with your current intervention or make a change.

The following examples are designed to illustrate when intervention changes should be made (making decisions regarding what type of change should be made will be discussed in the section to follow). Also keep in mind that **before changing an intervention, you should first ensure that the program is being implemented correctly.**

Stable Responding at Zero

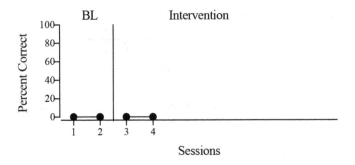

In the graph above, we see that the learner has zero levels of correct responding across two sessions of intervention. These data indicate that the individual is either not responding at all or responding incorrectly, both of which are problematic because the individual is either not contacting reinforcement and/or is practicing errors. Therefore, it would be important to **make a change** to your intervention without waiting to see what happens if you run a few more sessions.

Take a moment now to think about your learners. Do you have any learners who are not responding with any accuracy, but no changes have been made?

Low, Stable Responding

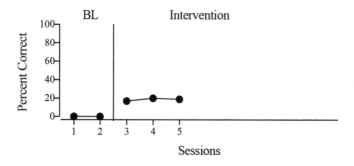

In the graph above, although correct responding is higher than baseline levels of responding, levels of responding are low across three sessions of intervention. These data indicate that the individual is either not responding frequently or is often responding incorrectly, both of which are problematic because the individual is either not contacting sufficient reinforcement and/or is often practicing errors. Therefore, it would be important to **make a change** to your intervention.

Take a moment now to think about your learners. Do you have any learners who are responding with very low accuracy, but no changes have been made?

Moderate, Stable Responding

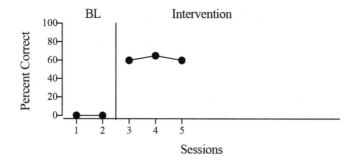

In the graph above, we see that the learner is sometimes responding correctly, but not often enough. These data indicate that the individual is either sometimes not responding or is sometimes responding incorrectly, both of which are problematic because the individual is either not contacting sufficient reinforcement and/or is practicing errors. Therefore, it would be important to **make a change** to your intervention.

Take a moment now to think about your learners. Do you have any learners who are responding with some accuracy, but no changes have been made?

High, Stable Responding

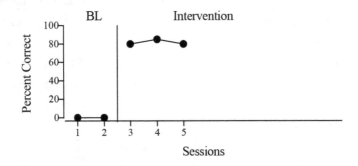

In the graph above, we see that the learner is often responding correctly, and responding is near mastery. These data indicate that the individual is rarely not responding or responding incorrectly, which is good because this means that the individual is either contacting reinforcement often and/or is rarely practicing errors. Therefore, you would want to **continue your intervention.** However, if no further progress is made after one or two more sessions, you would want to make a change to your intervention.

Take a moment now to think about your learners. Do you have any learners who have been responding with high levels of accuracy for many sessions, but no changes have been made?

Variable Responding (low, low, high)

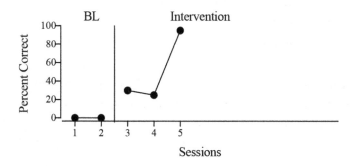

In the graph above, we see that the learner has just begun to respond correctly at mastery levels. These data indicate that the individual has now contacted high levels of reinforcement, which is good because this means that the individual is now more likely to exhibit the correct response and less likely to error. Therefore, you would want to **continue your intervention.** However, if progress does not continue after one or two more sessions, you would want to make a change to your intervention.

Take a moment now to think about your learners. Do you have any learners who have responded with high levels of accuracy, but progress did not continue, and no changes have been made?

Variable Responding (low, high, low)

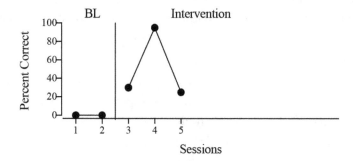

In the graph above, we see that the learner has responded with a high level of accuracy during only one session, and responding has decreased.

These data indicate that although the individual has contacted high levels of reinforcement, it was not sufficient to maintain behavior, which is problematic because the individual is practicing errors more often than the correct response. Therefore, you would want to **change your intervention.**

Take a moment now to think about your learners. Do you have any learners with few sessions of high levels of accuracy, but progress did not continue, and no changes have been made?

Variable Responding (high, low, high)

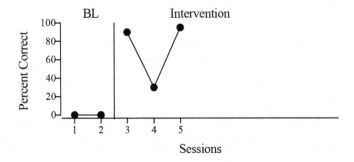

In the graph above, we see that the learner has responded at low levels during only one session of intervention. Given that the low level was observed only once, these data may indicate that some extraneous variable may have influenced that one session (e.g., illness), which is not too problematic because the individual is otherwise contacting reinforcement and rarely practicing errors. Therefore, you would want to **continue your intervention.** However, if you continue to see periodic low levels of responding, you would want to evaluate if something might be different during the sessions where correct responding is low (e.g., different instructor). If you are unable to determine a variable that is different during those sessions, you would want to make an intervention change.

Take a moment now to think about your learners. Do you have any learners who have had several dips in performance, and no analysis has been conducted nor have any changes been made?

Variable Responding (high, high, low)

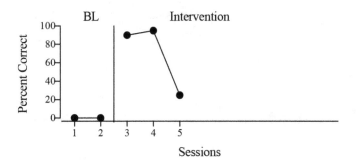

In the graph above, we see that the learner has responded at low levels during only one session of intervention. Given that the low level was observed only once, these data may indicate that some extraneous variable may have influenced that one session (e.g., illness), which is not too problematic because the individual is otherwise contacting reinforcement and rarely practicing errors. Therefore, you would want to **continue your intervention.** However, if you continue to see periodic low levels of responding, you would want to evaluate if something might be different during the sessions where correct responding is low (e.g., different instructor). If you are unable to determine a variable that is different during those sessions, you would want to make an intervention change.

Take a moment now to think about your learners. Do you have any learners who have had several dips in performance, and no analysis has been conducted nor have any changes been made?

Low, Shallow, Increasing Trend

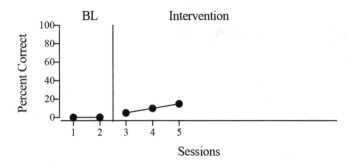

In the graph above, we see that although the learner's correct responding is increasing, responding is low and not increasing very quickly. These data indicate that the individual is not contacting a lot of reinforcement and is likely practicing errors; therefore, it is unlikely that progress will continue in an upward trend. Also consider that even if progress were to continue at the current rate, skill mastery will not be obtained for many more sessions. Therefore, an **intervention change should be made** in order to speed up learning.

Take a moment now to think about your learners. Do you have any learners whose progress is very slight, and no changes have been made to speed up learning?

Moderate, Shallow, Increasing Trend

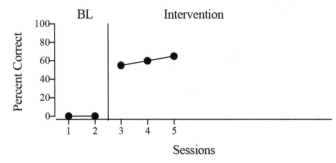

In the graph above, we see that although the learner's correct responding is increasing, responding is not increasing quickly. However, although responding is not increasing quickly, also consider that responding is approaching mastery levels. Therefore, **continuing the intervention and making a change would both be appropriate.** However, if you decide to continue the intervention, be sure to closely monitor the data as a change will need to be made if the increasing trend does not continue.

Take a moment now to think about your learners. Do you have any learners who had been making progress and were near mastery, however, progress has not continued, and no changes have been made?

High, Shallow, Increasing Trend

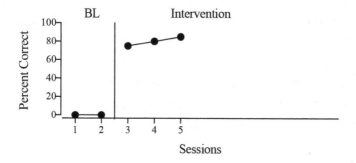

In the graph above, we see that although the learner's correct responding is not increasing quickly, correct responding is at or near mastery criteria. These data indicate that the individual is contacting reinforcement and rarely committing errors. Therefore, you should **continue the intervention.** However, be sure to closely monitor the data as a change will need to be made if high levels of responding are not maintained.

Take a moment now to think about your learners. Do you have any learners who had been making progress and were near mastery, however, progress has not continued, and no changes have been made?

Steep, Increasing Trend

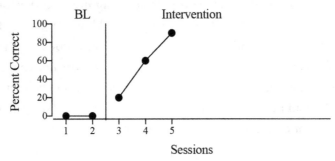

Sessions

In the graph above, we see that the learner's correct responding is increasing quickly. These data indicate that the individual is increasingly contacting more reinforcement and committing fewer errors. Therefore, you should **continue the intervention.** However, it will be important to closely monitor the data as a change will need to be made if high levels of responding are not maintained.

Take a moment now to think about your learners. Do you have any learners who had been making progress and were near mastery, however, progress has not continued, and no changes have been made?

Mild, Decreasing Trend from High Level

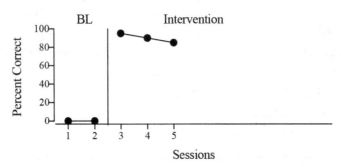

Sessions

In the graph above, we see that although the learner's correct responding is decreasing, the levels of correct responding are high, and the decrease is mild. These data indicate that the individual is contacting high levels of reinforcement and rarely committing errors. Therefore, you should **continue the intervention.** However, be sure to closely monitor the data as a change will need to be made if levels of correct responding continue to decrease across the next one or two sessions.

Take a moment now to think about your learners. Do you have any learners whose correct responding has continued to decrease, and no changes have been made?

Mild, Decreasing Trend from Moderate Level

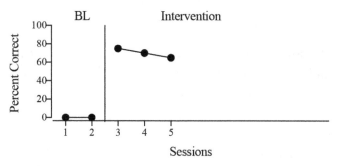

In the graph above, we see that although the learner's correct responding is not decreasing quickly, the levels of correct responding are only moderate. These data indicate that the individual is sometimes contacting reinforcement and sometimes committing errors or otherwise not responding. Therefore, you should **change your intervention** to regain higher levels of responding.

Take a moment now to think about your learners. Do you have any learners whose correct responding is only moderate and is decreasing, and no changes have been made?

Steep, Decreasing Trend

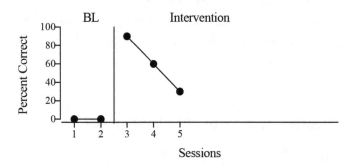

In the graph above, we see that although the learner's correct responding was high initially, it is now decreasing quickly. These data indicate that the individual is not contacting much reinforcement and beginning to commit more errors or otherwise not respond. Therefore, you should **change your intervention.**

Take a moment now to think about your learners. Do you have any learners whose correct responding started high and subsequently decreased, and no changes have been made?

ADDITIONAL CONSIDERATIONS

The previous content provides some basic suggestions for when to make program changes; however, it is also important to consider what your graph includes. For example, if your graph includes responding for several targets (e.g., 10 sight words), consider graphing each target individually so that you can see where the errors are occurring. Similarly, if you are graphing percent steps completed in a task analysis (e.g., handwashing), you may find it helpful to look at trial-by-trial data to determine which particular steps the learner is struggling with. In addition, a trial-by-trial analysis of the data may indicate prompts that have been successful and unsuccessful that can guide your decisions regarding program changes.

REVIEW

For each of the graphs below, determine whether a change should be made to the current intervention, or you should continue with the intervention in place. For each learner, assume the program is being implemented correctly.

Learner 1

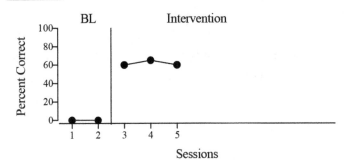

a. Make a change now

b. Continue the intervention

c. Both a and b would be appropriate

Learner 2

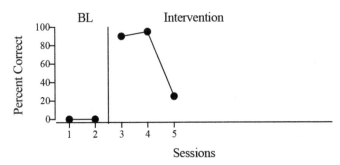

a. Make a change now

b. Continue the intervention

c. Both a and b would be appropriate

Learner 3

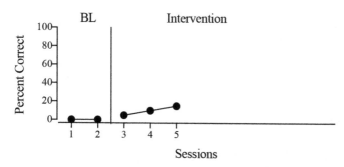

a. Make a change now

b. Continue the intervention

c. Both a and b would be appropriate

Learner 4

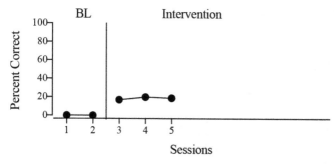

a. Make a change now

b. Continue the intervention

c. Both a and b would be appropriate

Learner 5

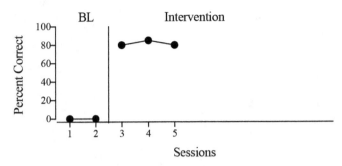

a. Make a change now

b. Continue the intervention

c. Both a and b would be appropriate

Learner 6

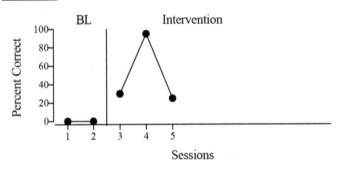

a. Make a change now

b. Continue the intervention

c. Both a and b would be appropriate

Learner 7

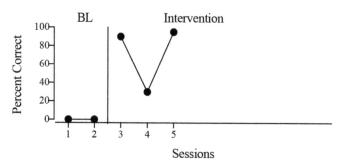

a. Make a change now

b. Continue the intervention

c. Both a and b would be appropriate

Learner 8

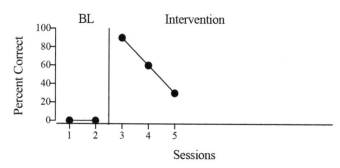

a. Make a change now

b. Continue the intervention

c. Both a and b would be appropriate

Learner 9

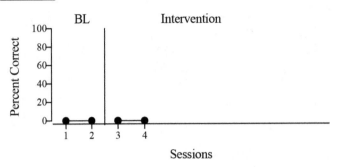

a. Make a change now
b. Continue the intervention
c. Both a and b would be appropriate

Learner 10

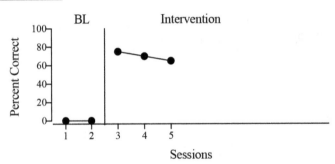

a. Make a change now
b. Continue the intervention
c. Both a and b would be appropriate

Learner 11

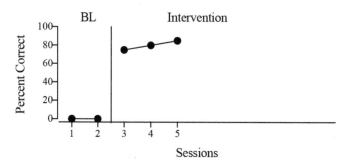

a. Make a change now

b. Continue the intervention

c. Both a and b would be appropriate

Learner 12

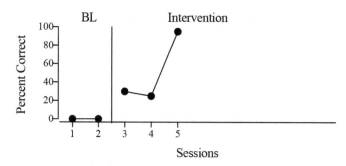

a. Make a change now

b. Continue the intervention

c. Both a and b would be appropriate

Learner 13

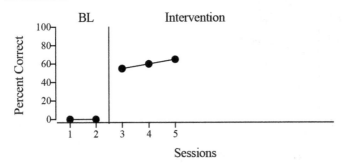

a. Make a change now

b. Continue the intervention

c. Both a and b would be appropriate

Learner 14

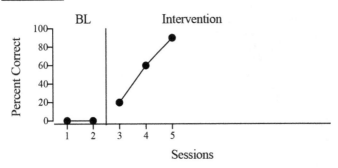

a. Make a change now

b. Continue the intervention

c. Both a and b would be appropriate

Learner 15

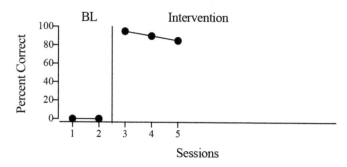

a. Make a change now

b. Continue the intervention

c. Both a and b would be appropriate

PART 4

MAKING PROGRAM CHANGES

EVERY DECISION WE MAKE FOR OUR LEARNERS is an important one, and making the wrong decision can be costly; therefore, learning how to make good program changes is critical for the success of the individuals with whom we work. Several factors should influence the decisions we make regarding changing aspects of a learner's program. You first want to determine if the learner is or is not making progress (see the previous section on Data-based Decision Making). If the learner is making progress, you need to determine if the level of progress is, or is not yet, at mastery, and whether prompts are being used to increase performance. If the learner is not making progress, you need to determine whether the lack of progress is due to lack of motivation (i.e., the learner *can* do it, but *won't*) or a true skill deficit (i.e., the learner can't perform the skill correctly).

In this section, you will learn what changes can be made to maximize correct responding and minimize errors.

LEARNER IS MAKING PROGRESS

If the learner is making progress and has **not yet met mastery,** continue teaching the skill.

If the learner is making progress and **has met levels of mastery *with prompts,*** either remove the prompt completely to allow for independence or decrease the intrusiveness of the prompt or how often you prompt.

If the learner is making progress and **has met levels of mastery *without prompts:***

- Fade reinforcement
- Transition from primary to conditioned reinforcers
- Discontinue teaching
- Assess for generalization
- Assess for stimulus equivalence
- Schedule maintenance checks

In the next section, the above points will be discussed more in detail, but mark this page for future reference.

Continuing Teaching

If the learner is making progress, continue teaching until the learner reaches mastery criteria. Keep in mind that **mastery criteria should be determined on an individual basis, NOT standardized across all learners.** Some learners may retain skills after achieving only 80% accuracy, and others may require an accuracy of 90% or even 100%. In addition, some learners may retain skills after achieving accuracy during one session, and others may require several consecutive sessions before skills should be considered mastered. The lowest accuracy and fewest number of sessions at accuracy should be used for determining mastery criteria for each learner so that the time spent teaching can be maximized.

Removing Prompts

When working with individuals who have difficulty learning, prompts can be very useful for evoking the correct response; in this way, the learner is contacting reinforcement and practicing the correct response more often. However, when prompts are used for too long, the learner may become dependent on the prompts. Therefore, once you are observing high levels of correct responding with prompts (several consecutive trials or sessions), remove the prompts to allow for the behavior to come under the control of the instruction alone. For some learners, you may find it useful to decrease the intrusiveness or frequency of the prompt before removing it completely. For example, if you are using a full physical prompt, first transition to a partial physical prompt. If you are currently only using a partial prompt, try interspersing opportunities for independence immediately following prompted trials instead of removing the prompt altogether (three consecutive prompted trials, then an unprompted trial). If the learner is not responding correctly when removing the prompt on subsequent trials, try removing the prompt immediately following error correction (see page 37).

Fading Reinforcement

For most learners, using schedules of reinforcement that are a high density (Fixed Ratio 1 [FR1]; the reinforcer is delivered following each correct response) can be extremely effective for teaching new skills. However, these dense schedules of reinforcement are not usually representative of what occurs in the natural environment. Therefore, reducing how often the learner is earning a reinforcer can be useful for ensuring the skill continues to be used when it is no longer part of a formal teaching session. When fading the reinforcement, be sure that the change is gradual. For example, you might reinforce three correct responses consecutively, then skip a reinforcer for the fourth correct response. The end goal is to make reinforcer delivery unpredictable.

Transitioning to Conditioned Reinforcers

Another common teaching strategy is to use primary (or natural) reinforcers, such as edible items and tablets. These items are potent rewards that don't require training; that is, the learner naturally likes these items. Although these items are very effective, similar to the point above, they are not likely going to be part of the learner's natural environment, which may decrease the likelihood that the learner will exhibit the skill outside of the formal teaching session. Therefore, it is important to ensure that the skill will occur with other reinforcers such as tokens (e.g., coins, stickers) and social interactions (e.g., praise, tickles, and high-fives). When transitioning to conditioned reinforcers, start by presenting the primary reinforcer and the conditioned reinforcer at the same time, and if using tokens, teach token trading before using tokens as a reinforcer so that the individual learns the value of a token. *Note: When teaching token trading, be sure to start with only one token.*

Discontinuing Teaching

We've already discussed determining mastery criteria; however, sometimes skills continue to be run after this point because an instructor doesn't have any new programs to run or because the data were not up to date on the graph, and sometimes skills do not need to be run for this many days/sessions. Therefore, you first want to be sure to have additional targets ready for the learner's instructor so that when a target is mastered, he is able to start a new target. Continuing to run targets for many sessions after mastery takes valuable time away from the learner learning new skills. Second, as mentioned earlier, consider whether it is necessary to have high accuracy for 3 consecutive days/sessions or whether you might master at 1 or 2 days/sessions. Mastering targets early is beneficial as it allows the learner to work on more targets sooner; however, take caution when reducing mastering criteria to ensure the learner is maintaining the skill at 1-week and 1-month probes.

Assessing for Generalization

Most skills are taught with one instruction, one person, with one stimulus, and in one setting, and this can be problematic because the learner learns to respond correctly only when all of these conditions are in place. For example, a learner may have been taught to select a red block in an array of items when asked to "Touch red", but is then unable to select the red block when asked to "Show me red" or is unable to select a different red item when asked to "Touch red." These are problems that often stem from poor instructional setups; however, the problems often go unnoticed because goals are mastered, and generalization is not assessed. Therefore, it is important to ensure that you check for generalization as soon as a skill is mastered. To check for generalization, **try using a different instruction or materials, having a different person present the instruction, and try assessing the skill in a different setting.** It is not valuable for a learner to exhibit a skill correctly only in the presence of the primary instructor, when a specific instruction is delivered, with only one stimulus, or in only one teaching setting. The skill will only be useful if it is generalized.

Assessing for Stimulus Equivalence

When conducting an initial assessment with a learner, it is common to assess many skills at once. For example, an instructor may evaluate a learner's ability to select an object when told the name of the object (i.e., receptive labeling) and also say the name of an object when the object is presented to the learner (expressive labeling), and it may be that the learner does not possess either of these skills. However, upon teaching one of these skills, the learner may indirectly acquire a skill for which no direct training was provided. For example, you may teach a learner to select the picture of a dog from an array when you say, "Find the dog", and then the learner (without direct training) may be able to say, "dog" when asked, "What is this?" in the presence of the picture of the dog. Therefore, before introducing new programs, it is important to assess for new skills that may have emerged since the initial assessment, so that you don't spend time writing and implementing programs for skills which the learner now possesses.

Scheduling Maintenance Checks

Although the primary goal of skill acquisition is mastery, the secondary goal is retention of the skill across time. If a skill has been learned but is not able to be recalled at a later point in time, it is much less useful to the learner. Therefore, as soon as a skill is mastered, it is important to schedule at least one maintenance check. Maintenance checks can occur any time following mastery of a skill (e.g., 1 week, 1 month), but should be done consistently. If during a maintenance check, the learner is unable to perform the skill correctly, the skill should be reintroduced for teaching. Also important is to avoid interspersing mastered targets with acquisition targets while a mastered target is in maintenance so that the learner is not practicing the mastered skill during the maintenance interval.

LEARNER IS NOT MAKING PROGRESS

When learners are not making progress, and you have ensured that a program is being implemented correctly, it is important to determine whether the learner is not making progress due to lack of motivation or because he is having difficulty performing the skill. Determining why the learner is not making progress should then help guide the decisions you make regarding program changes. Although making this determination can be difficult, one indicator that the learner is not motivated is when the learner is consistently not responding across several programs or not responding during difficult programs, and one indicator that the learner may be experiencing a skill deficit is when he is consistently making attempts but responding incorrectly. If you are unsure, you may consider revising your data collection to include recording a "no response" (indicated by NR) and record what type of errors are occurring across a few sessions.

Below are a few suggestions for addressing motivation and general skill deficits (specific skill deficits will be addressed in a subsequent section).

Addressing Motivation

- **Use a different reinforcer**
  If a learner is lacking progress across skills in most programs, it may be that you don't have a valuable reinforcer and need to find a completely different item to use as a reinforcer. One way to increase the likelihood of having a good reinforcer is to allow the learner to choose what he wants. This doesn't mean conducting a preference assessment once per week and using the two highest preferred items; this means allowing choices often throughout the session to capture current motivation. Another common change you might make to a reinforcer is to use a primary reinforcer in lieu of a conditioned reinforcer. That is, if your learner earns tokens for responding correctly, then trades those tokens for an edible or access to a leisure item, consider delivering the actual item following correct responding. Finally, you may want to try a completely different type of reinforcer. Common reinforcers

used are tablets, edibles, and tokens, and although delivery of these items requires little effort by the instructor, consider fun ways to interact with your learner (e.g., spinning, bouncing, running, hide-and-seek, etc.) that may re-capture motivation.

- **Give more of the reinforcer**

  Another change you might consider is increasing the amount of the reinforcer you are using. For example, if your learner earns one Skittle for each correct response for all targets in acquisition, consider delivering two or three for correct responses. Alternatively, you might consider delivering two different reinforcers in lieu of increasing the magnitude. For example, you could deliver one Skittle and 1 minute of access to a video on a tablet. Furthermore, the value of reinforcers might be increased if you pair two similar reinforcers. For example, delivering a chip and a sip of soda or delivering a toy train while playing a video about trains.

- **Reduce effort**

  Perhaps your learner has gotten to the point where he is working for 10 minutes straight before accessing reinforcers, or maybe the learner has to correctly respond 20 times before accessing reinforcers. In this case, you might take a few steps backward and decrease how long the learner has to work or how much work he has to complete before taking a break. In addition, perhaps you can reduce the difficulty of the task by providing assistance or working on a less effortful task.

- **Allow choices**

  In general, our learners often make very few choices about anything. Caregivers and staff make most decisions regarding what they will wear, eat, do, etc., which gives learners very little control over their daily life. In addition to allowing choices of reinforcers as previously mentioned, you might also consider allowing the learner to choose which work programs, targets, or order of tasks to give the learner some control over his environment.

- **Differentially reinforce**

  For learners who have become dependent on prompts and, therefore, wait for you to provide the correct response, consider removing the reinforcer for prompted responses and only delivering the reinforcer for independent responses to increase the likelihood they will respond independently.

- **Ensure immediate delivery of the reinforcer**

  Take a moment to re-evaluate the immediacy of the reinforcer delivery. It may be that the learner is not associating working with access to reinforcement because of a delay between a response and delivery of a reinforcer. Consider that even though you, as the instructor, are responding immediately after the learner's response by grabbing the tablet or edible item, there may be a delay when you have to turn on or unlock the tablet, break a piece of edible, etc.

- **Deliver reinforcer for free**

  If a learner has not been contacting reinforcement due to incorrect or lack of responding on difficult skills, it may be helpful to deliver a few reinforcers for free prior to the delivery of the instruction.

- **Consider when to implement each program**

  When a learner has a variety of programs, you should think about when you are implementing the programs. For example, if a learner has programs for which he primarily earns food reinforcers, you don't want to run those programs after a meal. Similarly, if a learner has free access to his iPad after school, you don't want to schedule sessions for 1 hour after school, during which time the learner has had continuous access to the reinforcer. Furthermore, if some programs are more difficult than others, try to avoid running those programs a) back-to-back, b) when the learner is currently engaging in or is demonstrating precursors to problem behavior, c) when a learner is sick/tired, and d) at the end of a long session.

Addressing General Skill Deficits

- **Use immediate prompts more often**

  In many cases, you have a valuable reinforcer, but the learner is still having difficulty correctly exhibiting the skill. When the skill is difficult for the learner, first consider increasing the amount of prompting. That is, if you are only prompting during error correction or prompting per the guidelines outlined previously, consider prompting for several consecutive trials or even an entire session or two depending on the learner.

- **Increase the intrusiveness of the prompt**

  Another change you might make is to increase the level of intrusiveness of the prompt. For example, if you are using a partial vocal prompt, consider using a full vocal prompt until the learner has more success engaging in the correct form of the response.

- **Change the type of prompt**

  Next, consider changing the type of prompt. For example, if you are using a point prompt to try to get the learner to touch a stimulus in an array, but the learner is not attending to your prompt, consider using a physical prompt or reducing the array of stimuli. Remember that the ultimate goal is to increase the frequency with which the learner is practicing the correct response, so continue trying different prompts until you find one that reliably evokes the correct form of the behavior.

- **Reinforce prompted responding**

  If you are using differential reinforcement by delivering the reinforcer only for correct independent responses, consider delivering the reinforcer for prompted responses so that the individual is contacting reinforcement. If your learner begins to rely on prompts, you may want to choose reinforcers of lesser value to deliver following prompted responses to maintain the value of independent responding.

- **Increase learning opportunities**
  If a learner is continuing to struggle with a specific target or targets within a program, decrease the number of trials you are working on easier targets so that you can increase the number of trials for working on more challenging skills.

- **Decrease number of program targets**
  Another consideration if the learner is having difficulty learning is that there might be too many programs or targets overall. If you suspect this might be the case, consider reducing the number of programs or targets until the learner is successfully learning a few skills.

- **Ensure immediate delivery of the reinforcer**
  In addition to choosing appropriate reinforcers, it is equally important that the reinforcer is delivered immediately. This will allow the learner to understand the relationship between correct responding and access to preferred items and activities and increase the likelihood that the learner will correctly perform the skill.

- **Differentially reinforce**
  If you are already using a primary reinforcer, you might consider removing that reinforcer for easier tasks such that the learner can only gain access to the most valuable reinforcer by responding correctly to the difficult skill. This will involve the identification of several reinforcers, but it may decrease the likelihood of satiation as well as increase the value of the reinforcer because access will be decreased. Also consider removing the reinforcer for prompted responses and only delivering the reinforcer for independent responses.

- **Use different teaching stimuli**
  In some cases, it may be that the target responses are too similar (teaching identification of W and V or cat and dog at the same time) which is making discrimination difficult for the learner. If

your distractor or other target stimuli are very similar, it might be useful to change the teaching stimuli or targets.

- **Break the skill down into smaller parts**
  Some skills are more complicated than other skills in that the skill requires several other skills to complete. If it is possible to reduce the complexity of the skill, consider working on approximations to the target response. For example, if a learner is learning to blow bubbles, this requires both a puckering of the lips and an exhale of breath. Therefore, you might work on these skills individually first, then work toward combining them.

- **Ensure necessary prerequisites are in the repertoire**
  It is also important to ensure that the learner has the necessary prerequisite skills for complex skills. For example, if a learner is struggling with addition, be sure that he can identify numbers and count before working on addition. Even if the prerequisite skill was mastered at some point in time, it may be helpful to revisit those skills.

- **Discontinue teaching the skill**
  Finally, consider the importance of the skill. When learners are not making progress after several program changes have been made, working on that skill is taking the place of working on other skills, and as the instructor, you need to determine if it is worth the learner's time to continue trying to teach the skill. In some cases, you may conclude that the skill is not critical and decide to discontinue teaching the skill even though it has not been mastered.

TROUBLESHOOTING SPECIFIC PROBLEMS

Several circumstances can arise during individualized instruction that require specific program modifications based on the type of error and skill type for which the error is occurring. In the next section, a variety of common learner challenges will be discussed as well as potential solutions for decreasing errors and increasing correct responses. Challenges to be discussed include prompt dependency, lack of attending, difficulty with specific skills, errors due to learning history, and intentional errors.

Prompt Dependency

One of the most common difficulties that occurs is prompt dependency, and strategies for decreasing prompt dependency vary depending on the type of prompt being used. Outlined below are suggestions for decreasing prompt dependency for each type of prompt.

- **Dependent on physical prompt**
  If you find that your learner is relying on physical guidance to correctly perform a skill (holds hands out for you to assist or otherwise waits for your prompt):
  - Try to **fade out the physical prompt across back-to-back teaching trials** by presenting your instruction with a full physical prompt (hand over hand), then immediately present the instructions again with something slightly less than a full physical and continue until you are not using a prompt.

  - Another way to fade out the physical prompt is to **slowly remove the full physical prompt within a trial.** That is, once you have established the correct form of the behavior (e.g., the learner is clapping) with full physical guidance, remove some of the physical prompts while the learner is engaging in the behavior. For example, while you are modeling touching nose and holding the learner's hand to his nose, slowly let go of the learner's hand. If the learner moves his hand off his nose, place it back on his nose, and try again to let go of his hand. When the learner keeps his hand on his nose independently, deliver a reinforcer.

- **Dependent on model prompt**
  If you find that your learner is waiting until you provide a model prompt:

  - Try **physically prompting from behind.** For example, if you are delivering the instruction *touch head*, have a second person stand behind the learner to remove the dependency on the visual prompt (i.e., model), and use the prompt fading guidelines above as needed.

- **Dependent on point prompts**
  If your learner has become dependent on point prompts when selecting one stimulus from an array, there are several different types of prompts that reduce dependency on the point prompt:

  - First, as mentioned in the previous point, you can **try using a physical prompt and fading.**

  - Second, you can **reduce the response options to one stimulus** and wait for the learner to respond.

  - Third, you can **try blocking incorrect responses,** which will force scanning and selecting.

  - Fourth, you can **increase the size of the target stimulus** and systematically fade the size to match that of the other stimuli as the learner is successful.

  - Fifth, you can **use a positional prompt** by placing the target stimulus closer to the learner than the non-target stimuli.

  - Finally, you can **use blank cards for the non-target stimuli** and systematically fade in the presence of similar stimuli;

alternatively, you can use non-target stimuli that are very different from the target stimulus. For example, if your target stimulus is a sight word, you can use pictures as the distractor stimuli.

Lack of Attending

Several problems related to attending often arise during individualized instruction. First, a learner may not attend to the instructor during the delivery of the instruction or while modeling a response. Second, a learner may not scan an array of stimuli before making a response. Third, a learner may respond by pointing to or touching a stimulus without looking at the stimulus to which he is responding. Outlined below are suggestions for addressing each of these challenges if removing distractions from the environment is not possible or has not been successful.

- **Lack of attending to the instructor**
  When a learner is not attending to an instructor, and it is important that he do so (e.g., if the instructor is trying to teach imitation):

  - **Briefly put the program on hold and reinforce attending.** That is, instead of making the reinforcer contingent on correct responding to the instruction, make the reinforcer contingent on attending to the instructor. See Essential Skills in Part 1.

- **Not scanning an array of stimuli**
  When a learner is not scanning an array of stimuli, then before delivering the target instruction (e.g., "Point to the dog"):

  - **Deliver the instruction to "look here" while pointing at one of the stimuli** and repeat this procedure for all stimuli in the array. After the learner has looked at each stimulus in the array, then present your target instruction (e.g., "Point to the dog").

- **Have the learner point to each stimulus.** After the learner has pointed to each stimulus in the array while looking at the stimuli, then present your target instruction (e.g., "Point to the dog").

- For learners who tend to have lower levels of compliance, you may find that **reinforcing the orienting response** is necessary. That is, deliver a reinforcer following compliance for looking at the stimulus.

- **Lack of attending to a specific stimulus**
  In some cases, a learner will scan an array but then respond by touching a stimulus without looking at it. Sometimes this behavior is shaped up because the learner intermittently contacts reinforcers for correct selections.

  - One way to increase the likelihood of looking at the stimulus is to **withhold providing consequences for responses that occur when the learner is not looking at the stimulus** while making a selection.

  - In addition, you should try **blocking the learner from looking at the distracting items,** and when possible, remove the distracting item.

Difficulty with Specific Skills

Learners are generally working on a variety of skills (e.g., manding, tacting, and imitation), and it may be that some of these skills are more difficult than others, in which case you see acquisition for some skills and not others. Outlined below are some suggestions for troubleshooting errors with specific types of skills.

- **Difficulty with multi-step instructions (imitative)**

  When you tell a learner, "Do this" and perform multiple actions (e.g., clapping, waving, and touching your head), and the learner does not imitate all actions or is performing the actions out of sequence, a few strategies may be helpful.

  - First, **ensure that the learner is waiting to start the sequence** until you have completed delivery of instructions by blocking any attempts to start early.

  - Second, you might **try pairing the model with a descriptive vocal cue.** Using the example above, while demonstrating the movements, you would say, "Clap, wave, touch head."

  - If a vocal cue is not successful, you might also **have the learner repeat the series of actions before performing the actions** (saying, "Clap, wave, head"); in this way, the learner may be able to provide a self-prompt. If providing the vocal cue is successful, you might then fade to using just a number (i.e., "1, 2, 3" while performing the actions) to reduce the prompting from specific to just a cue for how many actions are in the series.

  - Another strategy is to **build the sequence of actions.** Using the example above, you would first say, "Do this" and only perform one action (i.e., clapping your hands), then you would repeat the instruction and perform the first and second actions (i.e., clapping your hands, then waving), and finally, you would repeat the instruction and perform all actions.

  - Finally, the **use of objects** may help facilitate imitation of all actions. That is, instead of abstract movements (e.g., waving), place three objects in front of the learner, demonstrate actions with the objects, then have the learner try to imitate. Fade use of objects on subsequent trials by including two actions with objects and the last without, then the first action with an object and last two without, until you are no longer using objects.

- **Difficulty with multi-step instructions (receptive)**
  When you tell a learner, "Show me how you clap your hands, wave, and touch your head," and the learner does not perform all the steps or is performing the steps out of sequence, a few strategies may be helpful.

  - First, **try simplifying your instruction** by reducing the verbiage. In the example above, say, "Clap, wave, touch head."

  - Next, **try modeling the actions.**

  - Next, **try building the sequence of steps** (see imitative on the previous page).

  - Another strategy is to **use objects** (see imitative on the previous page).

  - Finally, **ensure the learner is waiting until you have presented all steps of the instruction** (see imitative on the previous page).

- **Difficulty with motor movements**
  Motor movements are often difficult for a variety of reasons. First, the movements are sometimes complex. Second, the learner often can't see the movement he is doing (touching his head or sticking out his tongue). Third, if the movement is a fine motor movement, this may be difficult due to the dexterity required to perform the skill. To aid a learner's success with motor movements:

  - You might **try using objects to create biofeedback.** For example, if trying to get a pucker or sticking out the tongue, have the learner push his lips against an object or reach for an object with his tongue. In another example, if trying to get the learner to press his lips together, touch a tongue depressor to the bottom lip so that the top lip will contact the novel stimulus when reaching the bottom lip. If teaching a gross motor movement such as raising arms, have the learner reach up and touch a bar.

- If the skill is complex, **work on approximations** to the target skill. That is, reinforce behaviors that are close to or part of the skill you are working toward.

- Another strategy is to **use a mirror to create visual feedback.** In this way, the learner is able to see when the movement he is doing is matching the movement you are modeling.

- Next, **using a clicker or other auditory signal to mark the target behavior** is helpful for clearly indicating to the learner when the correct form of the behavior has occurred.

- Finally, **consulting with a Speech Language Pathologist, Physical Therapist, or Occupational Therapist** may be helpful.

- **Difficulty with intraverbals**
  Learners who are beginning to work on intraverbals often have a strong echoic repertoire due to prerequisite training. Although it's necessary for a learner to have an echoic repertoire to be able to learn intraverbals, the learner often errors by repeating the instruction. For example, when teaching the response "Go", the learner says, "Ready, set" following delivery of the instruction, "Ready, set..." When this occurs, there are several strategies you might try.

  - One strategy is to **first establish the correct response (i.e., "Go") as an echoic** (i.e., say, "Say, go"), then systematically add in the instruction quietly and maintain a loud echoic prompt. For example, say, "ready, set, say, GO." Then, as the learner is responding correctly, systematically increase the volume of the instruction.

  - Another useful strategy is to **use a visual prompt to cue the target response.** Your visual cue can be a card with the target word on it or even a blank, colored card. Using your visual cue, teach the learner to respond in the presence of the card.

For example, hold up the card while saying, "Say, go." When the learner has learned to say, "Go" in the presence of the card, quietly present your instruction as described before, then hold up the card when the learner is to respond. Then, as the learner is responding correctly, systematically increase the volume of the instruction.

- If using a visual is ineffective, or you don't have a visual stimulus handy, you might **try using a motor movement such as a hand clap.** This strategy would be carried out identically to the visual-prompt strategy; however, you will clap your hands instead of holding up a card.

- **Difficulty with echoics**
  Many learners have difficulty imitating sounds, and several factors should be considered when determining what program changes should be made.

  - First, **ensure that the target sounds are developmentally appropriate.** It may be the case that the sound you are working on with your 3-year-old learner is one that is sometimes not developed until 5 years old with typically developing children, in which case you can put the skill on hold or choose another target.

  - If you have determined that the target sound is appropriate, also **ensure that the learner can display the correct corresponding oral motor movement** without the vocalization. For example, if you are trying to get the learner to say, "oo" (as in "smooth"), ensure that the learner can pucker his lips.

  - In addition, you can try **adding a hand cue/movement** with the target sound. If you want to use hand cues for multiple sounds, be sure to use a different hand cue for each sound.

  - If the echoic involves more than one syllable, first **ensure that the learner can imitate each sound in isolation** then build in sequence (first sound, first and second sound blended, then all three sounds blended together). Another option is to **use visual markers for each syllable or word** by laying out blank cards or objects that can be touched as you prompt the learner to repeat the sounds.

- Finally, **consult with a Speech Language Pathologist** for additional tips.

- **Difficulty with eye contact**

  Lack of eye contact is very common among learners and is often one of the most difficult skills to acquire. A few strategies are listed below.

  - A common strategy for getting the initial orientation of the eyes toward a person's face is to **hold a preferred stimulus in front of your eyes;** however, it is often difficult to fade out use of the object.

  - Another strategy is to **use a clicker to mark the occurrence of eye contact** as this skill may not be discrete/salient for all learners. To do this, press the clicker the moment the learner makes eye contact.

  - It is also important to **ensure that reinforcement is being delivered immediately.**

  - **Reinforcing several instances of eye contact in a row** can also be beneficial. To do this, select a period of time (e.g., 10 or 15 minutes) during which you will work on only eye contact and reinforce every instance of eye contact (either spontaneous or following an instruction to look).

  - Finally, consider **blocking looking away,** particularly if the learner is looking at something specific.

- **Difficulty with receptive identification**
  - See section on prompt dependency and lack of attending.
  - Consider medical evaluation for vision problems.

Errors Due to Learning History

Sometimes we think our learner isn't learning because he keeps engaging in the same incorrect response, such as always selecting the target on the left or consistently engaging in one target behavior prior to another (e.g., when asked to touch his head, the learner claps first then touches his head, or when asked to point to the picture of a dog in an array, the learner first touches other stimuli before touching the picture of the dog). Although the learner isn't responding in the way that we want him to respond, these behaviors indicate teaching errors. That is, the learner has experienced reinforcement for these errors and has, in a sense, learned to error.

- **Positional biases**
  As good practice, instructors are taught to vary the position in which target stimuli are placed in an array. That is, in an array of three stimuli, sometimes the target stimulus is placed on the left, sometimes on the right, and other times in the center; and the number of times the card is in each position is approximately equal. Although this is a good idea in general and effective for reducing positional biases for most learners, two problems can occur. First, if the teaching procedure is done correctly (as outlined above), the learner will intermittently contact reinforcement when only selecting targets in one position (33% of the time), which can maintain positional responding. Second, sometimes, the teaching procedure is not done correctly. That is, the instructor puts the target stimulus in a specific position more often than other positions, which can happen due to the reinforcement of instructor behavior. For example, if putting the stimulus on the

left results in more correct responding, the instructor may be more likely to put the stimulus on the left because correct learner responding is functioning as a reinforcer for instructor behavior. To address positional biases:

- You want to **systematically place target stimuli away from the position the learner continues to select.** For example, if the learner consistently selects the card on the left, only place the target stimulus on the right. When the learner is responding correctly on the right, move the target stimulus to the left. Continue to do this until positional biases are no longer present.

- Another option is to **change the array.** For example, if the individual is choosing the stimulus in the middle of three, add a fourth card to remove the middle. In another example, if the learner is consistently selecting the stimulus on one side (far left or far right), change your array to a vertical display to eliminate left and right sides.

- **Scrolling**

  Scrolling is another common problem that occurs due to accidental teaching error. Because the instructor's goal is for the learner to respond correctly, the instructor is not always quick to correct errors, but rather gives the learner another chance to respond correctly. Although waiting for a correct response increases the likelihood that a learner will respond correctly, and it seems fair to give the learner another chance, this teaches the learner to try a variety of behaviors. To decrease scrolling:

  - You might first **conduct several trials during which you immediately prompt the correct response** so that the learner has practice with performing only the correct response.

  - Next, it will be important to either **physically block scrolling behavior** or immediately remove stimuli and represent the instruction with a prompt.

- **Repeated use of mastered responses**

  Often you will see a learner engage in previously mastered responses when presenting a new, but similar instruction. For example, you may have taught a learner to touch his head, and now when you say, "Touch nose," the learner is touching his head. This is usually because the only target the learner was working on that included the word *touch* was "Touch head" and has learned to touch his head when hearing the word *touch*. This is also common with motor imitation. A learner is taught to clap his hands when hearing, "Do this," and then when a new motor movement is introduced, the learner continues to clap his hands. When this occurs:

    - It is important to be sure to **work on more than one target within a given program** so that the learner has to attend to all parts of the instruction. For example, if you are teaching receptive colors, target two or more colors so that you will have multiple instructions that are similar "Show me [color]."

    - Alternatively, you might want to **temporarily discontinue teaching for that skill** so that the learner does not have the opportunity to continue practicing the incorrect response.

    - Another strategy to consider is **temporarily removing part of the instruction.** For example, if you are asking the learner to touch his head (i.e., "Touch head"), you can instead just say, "Head" until the learner learns to respond to the important part of the instruction. When the learner is responding correctly and independently, then you can add back in the other parts of the instruction.

Intentional Errors

Although most of the time learner errors are due to lack of attending or skill deficits, there are some instances where errors are intentional. That is, the correct response is in the learner's repertoire; however, the greater reinforcer is in the consequence for erroring (e.g., attention, error correction). If you have determined (or suspect) that the learner is erroring on purpose, several strategies may be useful.

- First, **discontinue error correction for that target** and simply move on to the next target without allowing another opportunity to respond. Doing this will remove attention following the error.

- Second, **have a high-value reinforcer available only for that target** such that the reinforcer cannot be earned for any other target, and as previously mentioned, only allow one opportunity.

- Third, if a learner has a timed work period, you might simply **stop the timer during errors,** such that the error is delaying the learner's access to break time (that includes preferred activities and attention).

- Finally, if the work period is response based (i.e., token earning), you might **use response cost** (i.e., token removal) contingent on errors so that more work will be required to earn the break.

REVIEW

What should you do if a learner is making progress and has met mastery levels with prompts?

1. _____

What should you do if a learner is making progress and has met mastery levels without prompts?

1. _____

2. _____

3. _____

4. _____

5. _____

6. _____

What changes can you make if the learner is not motivated?

1. _____

2. _____

3. _____

4. _____

5. _____

6. _____

7. _____

8. _____

What changes can make if the learner is generally having difficulty acquiring skills?

1. _____

2. _____

3. _____

4. _____

5. _____

6. _____

7. _____

8. _____

9. _____

10. _____

11. _____

What can you do if the learner is dependent on physical prompts?

1. _____

2. _____

What can you do if the learner is dependent on a model prompt?

1. _____

What can you do if the learner is dependent on point prompts?

1. _____

2. _____

3. _____

4. _____

5. _____

6. _____

What should you do if the learner is not attending to the instructor?

1. _____

What can you do if the learner is not scanning the array of stimuli?

1. _____

2. _____

3. _____

What can you do if the learner is not attending to a specific stimulus?

1. _____

2. _____

What can you do when a learner is having difficulty imitating a series of actions?

1. _____

2. _____

3. _____

4. _____

5. _____

What can you do when a learner is having difficulty following multi-step instructions?

1. _____

2. _____

3. _____

4. _____

5. _____

What can you do if a learner is having difficulty with motor movements?

1. _____

2. _____

3. _____

4. _____

5. _____

What can you do if a learner is repeating the instruction during intraverbal training?

1. _____

2. _____

3. _____

What can you do if a learner is having difficulty with echoics?

1. _____

2. _____

3. _____

4. _____

5. _____

What can you do if a learner is having difficulty with eye contact?

1. _____

2. _____

3. _____

4. _____

5. _____

What can you do if a learner has a positional bias?

1. _____

2. _____

What can you do if a learner is scrolling?

1. _____

2. _____

What can you do if a learner is repeating a mastered response?

1. _____

2. _____

3. _____

What can you do if a learner is intentionally responding incorrectly?

1. _____

2. _____

3. _____

4. _____

FINAL THOUGHTS

Always remember that the first goal is to get the learner engaging in the correct response, and if you are having difficulty, remember to use resources. Regardless of your training or experience, it is often helpful to consult with another professional within, or even outside, your discipline to gain insight from others who may have experienced similar challenges. In addition, be sure to stay current with the literature and attend conferences to maintain current best-practice standards. Using available resources will help ensure that you are providing the best services possible for each of your learners.

Part 1 Answer Key

Which skills are essential for any learner who will be learning new skills?

1. willingly approaches the instructor
2. accepts a limited amount of reinforcement without exhibiting problem behavior
3. relinquishes access to a preferred item with little problem behavior
4. waits for a reinforcer to be delivered without exhibiting problem behavior
5. attends to (looks at) the instructor and stimuli
6. waits for instructor without touching teaching materials
7. responds to a variety of prompts (e.g., gestural, model, physical) and does not exhibit problem behavior
8. is able to request preferred items and activities as well as to terminate a non-preferred activity
9. is able to comply with simple instructions

What should you consider when selecting a new skill?

1. Is the skill age appropriate?
2. Will the skill be useful for the learner?
3. Does the learner have the necessary prerequisite skills?
4. Is the skill a prerequisite skill for other important skills?
5. Is the skill important to the caregiver or learner?
6. Is the skill likely to be maintained in the natural environment?
7. Are the necessary resources available?

What should you consider when selecting skills for learners with intensive support needs?

1. Start basic independent living and self-care skills early
2. Discontinue academics with older children

3. Ensure a variety of leisure skills

What should you consider when selecting skills for individuals with minimal support needs?

1. Try to keep academic performance at the rate of peers
2. Start training for vocational skills before leaving high school
3. Ensure advanced independent living and self-care skills

What factors should influence how many skills you target?

1. Level of support needs
2. Number of hours of instruction per week
3. Level of compliance/interfering problem behavior
4. Number of programs
5. Instructor fluency
6. Length of each session
7. Difficulty of programs

Part 2 Answer Key

What basic session components should you include in your teaching sessions?

1. Have fun
2. Mix up your stimuli, praise, targets, etc.
3. Speak normally
4. Use common stimuli
5. Use learner-response-based prompting
6. Use an appropriate pace
7. Take breaks often
8. Deliver reinforcers immediately
9. Allow choice of reinforcers
10. Match the reinforcer with the response effort
11. Structure the environment

What are some things you just learned about how to use error correction, prompting, and reinforcement to maximize learning, and how might you incorporate these changes with some of your current learners?

In general, if the learner is responding correctly without a prompt, the instructor should continue to present the instruction without a prompt and work on other teaching targets. However, if the learner is responding incorrectly, the instructor should present a prompt during subsequent trials and provide learning opportunities often. Once the learner is responding with a prompt, the instructor should present only the instruction.

With respect to reinforcement, deliver reinforcers based on the learner's first response to a trial; if you allowed for independence, deliver the reinforcer only for an independent response; if you used an immediate prompt, deliver a reinforcer for correctly responding with a prompt. As the learner is acquiring the skill, reinforce only for independent responses. When a learner is practicing a new or challenging skill, deliver the reinforcer for prompted responses.

Which behaviors are important to record?

1. Learner responding (correct, incorrect, no response)
2. Instructor prompts

What are three ways to intersperse targets?

1. Rotating acquisition targets from the same program
2. Rotating acquisition targets from different programs
3. Rotating acquisition and mastered targets

What did you learn are the advantages of interspersing mastered targets?

1. Learner displays more correct responses
2. Learner earns more reinforcers

What did you learn are the disadvantages of interspersing mastered targets?

1. If reinforcement is being delivered for mastered targets, learner motivation to respond to acquisition targets may be reduced
2. Repeated presentation of mastered targets may become boring for the learner
3. Presentation of mastered targets creates extra work for the learner
4. Presenting mastered targets takes time away from working on acquisition targets

Part 3 Answer Key

Learner 1: Change
Type of responding: Stable (moderate)

Learner 2: Continue
Type of responding: Variable (high, high, low)

Learner 3: Change
Type of responding: Increasing trend (shallow, low)

Learner 4: Change
Type of responding: Stable (low)

Learner 5: Continue
Type of responding: Stable (high)

Learner 6: Change
Type of responding: Variable (low, high, low)

Learner 7: Continue
Type of responding: Variable (high, low, high)

Learner 8: Change
Type of responding: Decreasing trend (steep)

Learner 9: Change
Type of responding: Stable at zero

Learner 10: Change
Type of responding: Decreasing trend (mild from moderate)

Learner 11: Continue
Type of responding: Increasing trend (shallow, high)

Learner 12: Continue
Type of responding: Variable (low, low, high)

Learner 13: Change or continue
Type of responding: Increasing trend (shallow, moderate)

Learner 14: Continue
Type of responding: Increasing trend (steep)

Learner 15: Continue
Type of responding: Decreasing trend (mild from high)

Part 4 Answer Key

What should you do if a learner is making progress and has met mastery levels with prompts?

1. Remove the prompt completely to allow for independence or decrease the intrusiveness or frequency of the prompt

What should you do if a learner is making progress and has met mastery levels without prompts?

1. Fade reinforcement
2. Transition from primary to conditioned reinforcers
3. Discontinue teaching
4. Assess for generalization
5. Assess for stimulus equivalence
6. Schedule maintenance checks

What changes can you make if the learner is not motivated?

1. Use a different reinforcer
2. Give more of the reinforcer
3. Reduce the effort of the task
4. Allow choices
5. Differentially reinforce
6. Ensure immediate delivery of the reinforcer
7. Deliver the reinforcer for free
8. Change when sessions are being conducted or change the order of programs

What changes can you make if the learner is generally having difficulty acquiring skills?

1. Use immediate prompts more often
2. Increase the intrusiveness of the prompt
3. Change the type of prompt
4. Reinforce prompted responding
5. Increase learning opportunities
6. Decrease the number of program targets
7. Ensure immediate delivery of the reinforcer
8. Use different teaching stimuli
9. Break down the skill into smaller parts
10. Ensure the learner has the necessary prerequisites
11. Discontinue teaching the skill

What can you do if the learner is dependent on physical prompts?

1. Fade out the physical prompt across back-to-back trials
2. Slowly remove the physical prompt within a trial

What can you do if the learner is dependent on a model prompt?

1. Physically prompt from behind

What can you do if the learner is dependent on point prompts?

1. Switch to a physical prompt and fade
2. Reduce the response options to one stimulus
3. Block incorrect responding
4. Increase the size of the target stimulus
5. Use a positional prompt
6. Use blank cards for the non-target stimulus

What should you do if the learner is not attending to the instructor?

1. Briefly put the program on hold and reinforce attending

What can you do if the learner is not scanning the array of stimuli?

1. Prompt the learner to look at each stimulus
2. Have the learner point to each stimulus before presenting the instruction
3. Reinforce orienting to each stimulus

What can you do if the learner is not attending to a specific stimulus?

1. Withhold providing consequences for responses that occur when the learner is not looking at the stimulus
2. Block the learner from looking away

What can you do when a learner is having difficulty imitating a series of actions?

1. Ensure that the learner is waiting to start the instruction
2. Try pairing the model with a descriptive vocal cue
3. Have the learner repeat the series of actions before performing the actions
4. Build the sequence of actions
5. Use objects with actions

What can you do when a learner is having difficulty following multi-step instructions?

1. Simplify your instructions
2. Model the actions
3. Build the sequence of actions
4. Use objects with actions
5. Ensure the learner is waiting until you have presented all steps

What can you do if a learner is having difficulty with motor movements?

1. Use objects to create biofeedback
2. Target approximations for complex skills
3. Use a mirror to create visual feedback
4. Use a clicker to mark the target behavior
5. Consult with another professional

What can you do if a learner is repeating the instruction during intra-verbal training?

1. Establish the response as an echoic and fade in instruction
2. Use a visual prompt to cue the target response
3. Pair a motor movement with the target vocal response

What can you do if a learner is having difficulty with echoics?

1. Ensure that the target sounds are developmentally appropriate
2. Ensure that the learner can display the correct corresponding oral motor movement
3. Try adding a hand cue/movement
4. If echoic involves multiple syllables or words, ensure that the learner can imitate each sound in isolation and try using visual markers for each syllable or word
5. Consult with a Speech Language Pathologist

What can you do if a learner is having difficulty with eye contact?

1. Hold a preferred stimulus in front of your eyes
2. Use a clicker to mark the occurrence of eye contact
3. Ensure that reinforcement is being delivered immediately
4. Reinforce several consecutive instances of eye contact
5. Blocking looking away and remove distractions when possible

What can you do if a learner has a positional bias?

1. Systematically place target stimuli away from the position the learner continues to select
2. Change the array to vertical or to include additional stimuli

What can you do if a learner is scrolling?

1. Conduct several trials during which you immediately prompt the correct response
2. Block scrolling

What can you do if a learner is repeating a mastered response?

1. Be sure to work on more than one target
2. Temporarily discontinue teaching for that skill
3. Temporarily remove part of the instruction

What can you do if a learner is intentionally responding incorrectly?

1. Discontinue error correction
2. Have a high-value reinforcer available for correct responding
3. Stop work time contingent on errors
4. Use response cost

APPENDIX A

Essential Skills Checklist

Skill	Not Assessed	Learner was unable to demonstrate skill(s)	Learner demonstrated skill(s)
Willingly approaches the instructor			
Accepts limited amount of reinforcement without exhibiting problem behavior			
Relinquishes access to a preferred item with little problem behavior			
Waits for a reinforcer to be delivered without exhibiting problem behavior			
Attends to (looks at) the instructor and stimuli			
Waits for the instructor without touching teaching materials			
Responds to a variety of prompts (e.g., gestural, model, physical) and does not exhibit problem behavior			
Is able to request preferred items and activities as well as to terminate a non-preferred activity			
Is able to comply with simple instructions			

APPENDIX B

Suggested Readings

Ala'i-Rosales, S., & Zeug, N. (2010). Three important things to consider when starting intervention for a child diagnosed with autism. *Behavior Analysis in Practice, 3*, 54-55.

Ghezzi, P. M. (2007). Discrete trials teaching. *Psychology in the Schools, 44*, 667–679.

Ghezzi, P. M., & Rogers, V. R. (2011). Promoting generalization. In J. K. Luiselli (Ed.). *Teaching and behavior support for children and adults with autism spectrum disorder: A practitioner's guide* (pp. 179-186). Oxford University Press.

Grow, L., & LeBlanc, L. A. (2013). Teaching receptive language skills: Recommendations for instructors. *Behavior Analysis in Practice, 6*, 56-75.

Lerman, D. C., Dittlinger, L. H., Fentress, G., & Lanagan, T. (2011). A comparison of methods for collecting data on performance during discrete trial teaching. *Behavior Analysis in Practice, 4*, 53–62.

Leaf, J. B., Leaf, R., McEachin, J., Taubman, M., Ala'i-Rosales, S., Ross, R. K., Smith, T., & Weiss, M. J. (2016). Applied behavior analysis is a science and, therefore, progressive. *Journal of Developmental Disorders, 46*, 720-731.

Leaf, J. B., Leaf, J. A., Alcalay, A., Kassardjian, A., Tsuji, K., Dale, S., Ravid, D., Taubman, M., McEachin, J., & Leaf, R. (2016). Comparison of most-to-least prompting to flexible prompt fading for children with autism spectrum disorder. *Exceptionality, 24,* 109-122.

Leaf, J. B., Leaf, R., Alacalay, A., Leaf, J. A., Ravid, D., Dale, S., Kassardjian, A., Tsuji, K., Taubman, M., McEachin, J., & Oppenheim-Leaf, M. (2015). Utility of formal preference assessments for individuals diagnosed with autism spectrum disorder. *Education and Training in Autism and Developmental Disabilities, 50*, 119–212.

Leaf, J. B., Cihon, J. H., Leaf, R., McEachin, J., Taubman, M. (2016). A Progressive approach to discrete trial teaching: Some current guidelines. *International Electronic Journal of Elementary Education, 9*, 361-372.

LeBlanc, L. A., Dillon, C. M., & Sautter, R. A. (2009). Establishing mand and tact repertoires. In R. A. Rehfledt & Y. Barnes-Holmes (Eds.). *Derived relational responding: Applications for learners with autism and other developmental disabilities: A progressive guide to change* (pp. 79-108). New Harbinger Publications, Inc.

Schlosser, R. W., & Sigafoos, J. (2011). Augmentative and alternative communication. In J. K. Luiselli (Ed.). *Teaching and behavior support for children and adults with autism spectrum disorder: A practitioner's guide* (pp. 91-96). Oxford University Press.

Shillingsburg, M. A., Hansen, B., & Wright, M. (2019). Rapport building and instructional fading prior to discrete trial instruction: Moving from child-led play to intensive teaching. *Behavior Modification, 43,* 288-306.

Sigafoos, J., Schlosser, R. W., O'Reilly, M. F., & Lancioni, G. E. (2011). Verbal language and communication. In J. K. Luiselli (Ed.). *Teaching and behavior support for children and adults with autism spectrum disorder: A practitioner's guide* (pp. 97-103). Oxford University Press.

Sturmey, P. (2011). Discrete trial teaching. In J. K. Luiselli (Ed.). *Teaching and behavior support for children and adults with autism spectrum disorder: A practitioner's guide* (pp. 167-172). Oxford University Press.

Taylor, B. A., & Fisher, J. (2010). Three important things to consider when starting intervention for a child diagnosed with autism. *Behavior Analysis in Practice, 3,* 52–53.

Weiss, M. J., & Zane, T. (2010). Three important things to consider when starting intervention for a child diagnosed with autism. *Behavior Analysis in Practice, 3,* 58–60.

Vets, T. L., & Green, G. (2010). Three important things to consider when starting interventions for a child diagnosed with autism. *Behavior Analysis in Practice, 3,* 56–57.

CPSIA information can be obtained
at www.ICGtesting.com
Printed in the USA
LVHW080302160723
752386LV00010B/870